Sitting in the Fire

ALSO BY ARNOLD MINDELL

Dreambody
Working With The Dreaming Body
River's Way
The Dreambody In Relationships
City Shadows
Coma, Key To Awakening
Working On Yourself Alone
The Year I
The Leader As Martial Artist
The Shaman's Body

Sitting In The Fire

LARGE GROUP TRANSFORMATION
USING CONFLICT AND DIVERSITY

ARNOLD MINDELL

LAO TSE PRESS
PORTLAND, OREGON

First edition 1995

Printed in the United States of America

Design by Kate Jobe
Author photo by Steven Bloch

Library of Congress Cataloging-in-Publication Data

Mindell, Arnold
    Sitting in The Fire: Large Group Transformation Using Conflict and
    Diversity

    Bibliography
    Includes index.
ISBN:1-887078-00-2 (pbk.)
Library of Congress Catalog Card Number: 95-78176

Contents

Acknowledgments

THOUGH I HAVE WORKED with groups in many parts of the world my ideas are still limited by my nationality, gender, age and experience. Colleagues and friends have helped widen a white, middle-aged, American male's viewpoint to create a more global perspective for this book.

I especially want to thank the process work community of Portland, Oregon, for testing my material on politics, group process, abuse, racism and privilege under a variety of conditions, and the Global Process Institute for sponsoring the worldwork seminars.

For helping me understand racism, I want to credit: Arlene and Jean-Claude Audergon, Ruby Brooks, Jean Gilbert, John Johnson, David Jones, Diane Wong and Rita Shimmin. For insights into sexism and lesbian/gay issues: Julie Diamond, Sara Halprin, J.M. Emetchi, Rhea and Markus Marty. For orientation to the literature on abuse: Nisha Zenoff, Phyllis Tatum and Paula Lilley.

I am grateful to people from around the world who enabled me to apply my ideas in a variety of cultures: in

Athens, Anna Maria and Constantine Angelopoulos; in Bombay, Anuradha Deb and J. M. Revar; in Berlin, Gabriela Espenlaub; in Tokyo, Yukio Fujimi and Professor Ogawa; in Paraguay, Benno Glauser; in Portland, Joe Goodbread, Kate Jobe and Dawn Menken; in Moscow, Andre Gostev and Slava Tsapkin; in Bratislava, Anton Heretik; in London, Roger Housdon; in Nairobi, Moses Ikiugu; in Washington, D.C., John Johnson, Bob and Helen Pelikan, and Charles and Anne Simpkinson; in Belfast, Fr. Miles O'Reilly; in Canada, David Roomy; in Warsaw, Bogna Szymkiewicz and Tomasz Teodorcyz; and the process work communities of Australia, Berlin, and Warsaw.

Thanks also to those who played a part in editing this book for style and accuracy: Nasira Alma, Lane Arye, Tom Atlee, Peter Block, Julie Diamond, Leslie Heizer, Ursula Hohler, Max Schuepbach and Jim Spickard. I am indebted to Kate Jobe and Leslie Heizer for their work on the original edition from Lao Tse Press. Thanks to David Jones for the book's title.

My partner Amy Mindell co-led all of the events on which this book is based. She is the originator of the concept of metaskills, an idea that is integral to my presentation here. Amy supported every moment of this work, from helping me cope with the enormity of the task to assisting me in the clarification of the concepts.

Foreword

BEHIND THE WORLD'S MOST difficult problems are people—
groups of people who don't get along together. You can
blame crime, war, drugs, greed, poverty, capitalism or the
collective unconscious. The bottom line is that people
cause our problems.

My teachers told me to avoid large groups: they are
unruly and dangerous. The only way work can be done,
they maintained, was in small groups where law and
order prevail. But the world is not composed of docile little groups. Enforcing law and order can't be our only
strategy for resolving problems.

Many of us shudder at violence. We want to insist on
peaceful behavior: line up here, single file. Follow *Robert's
Rules of Order*. One person speak at a time. Finish one subject before moving on to the next.

Yet enforcing order does not stop riots, hinder war or
reduce world problems. It may even kindle the fire of
group chaos. If we don't permit hostilities a legitimate
outlet, they are bound to take illegitimate routes.

This book demonstrates that engaging in heated conflict instead of running away from it is one of the best ways to resolve the divisiveness that prevails on every level of society — in personal relationships, business and the world.

The pages that follow will introduce you to innerwork as a way to overcome the fear of conflict. You will gain understanding of the cultural, personal and historical issues that underlie multicultural violence. You will acquire some of the skills necessary to work with large groups of people.

The fire that burns in the social, psychological and spiritual dimensions of humanity can ruin the world. Or this fire can transform trouble into community. It's up to us. We can avoid contention, or we can fearlessly sit in the fire, intervene and prevent world history's most painful errors from being repeated. Process work, which will be described in Chapter One, refers to the creative utilization of conflict as "worldwork."

After I finished the first draft of this book, I had a dream that was set near the turn of the millennium. In a conference call, leaders of many cities were talking to one another. People in Vladivostok, Anchorage, Seattle, Chicago, Montreal, New York, London, Berlin, Helsinki, Stockholm, Warsaw and Moscow were saying, "We have tried everything else. Nothing has succeeded. Let's try this new worldwork. Let's open up to what is happening in communities. Perhaps we can begin a new world order." In my dream, people actually learned to work with one another.

In the real world today, though nations of the North have developed advanced telecommunication systems that connect all parts of the globe, people still can't communicate effectively when there is trouble. In the South, a background noise of muffled oppression complicates interactions and makes revolutions. This noise is the low roar of vengeance from people whose voices are neglected by the mainstreams of First World cultures. When the energy of those voices spills over, the results are called "riots" or "minority crime." People who support minority representation are often warned by those in power to change direction, as though conflict and latent violence would go away if only we ignored them. However, suppression leads to revolts and more unhappiness.

That's the essence of the old multicultural paradigm: deny the problems and they will go away. Avoid and punish those who rock the boat.

My dream foresaw the full emergence of a new paradigm that is already trying to break into mainstream consciousness. I hope that this book will inspire you to take part in the realization of that dream.

Part I

World History From Inside Out

1

Fire:
The Price of Liberty

CREATING FREEDOM, community and viable relationships has its price. It costs time and courage to learn how to sit in the fire of diversity. It means staying centered in the heat of trouble. It demands that we learn about small and large organizations, open city forums and tense street scenes. If you step into leadership or facilitatorship without this learning, you may spend your time recapitulating the blunders of history.

The new worldwork paradigm offers us a number of fresh perspectives:

Chaos: In worldwork, conflict and moments of chaos are valued within group process because these can quickly create a sense of community and a lasting organization.

Learning: Worldwork expects conflict to be our most exciting teacher.

Open Heart: Worldwork relies on heartfulness in order to sit in the fire of conflict and not be burned. Worldwork uses the fire's heat to create community.

Self-knowledge: Worldwork stresses recognition that we ourselves are part of every conflict around us. Worldwork utilizes self-awareness skills to become part of the solution.

The Unknown: Worldwork acknowledges that sustainable community has always been based on respect for the unknown.

To those who want sustainable organizations and communities, my advice is: begin by being humble. Go back to school. Learn awareness. Learn about rank. You will save yourself and your community a lot of pain.

Thomas Jefferson, a past president of the United States, might have agreed. The price of liberty, he said, is vigilance. But his idea of vigilance didn't include keeping a protective eye on diversity. As I define it, vigilance means awareness of the manifold ideas and feelings in yourself and in the world around you. This awareness is part of the price of democracy and peace. The rest is learning skills to deal with personal, ethnic and international disputes.

There is more to democracy than awareness and the courage when necessary to sit in the fire. But few of us are willing to pay even this minimum price. Who likes to deal with anger and threats? Yet organizations must learn to handle chaos and complexity if we are to survive increasingly rapid change. If one person in one hundred will pay the price, our cities and world will evolve faster than we believe possible. Riots and wars will be less needed.

Many of us would like the world to change, but we don't want to endure the trouble of helping make that happen. It's easier to dream of better leaders who give charismatic speeches about community or civil rights, decreases or increases in military and police protection, improvements in the economy and the betterment of humankind. Communism dreams of reducing class distinctions and economic exploitation. Democracy dreams of equality and human rights. Spiritual traditions encourage us to love one another. Some of us hope society will outgrow power and class structures. Others think people should be good rather than evil, giving and not greedy.

On the whole, our visions indicate that we distrust human beings and wish they were different. Businesses and individuals alike resolve, "Our interests first and others second, and then only if they support our goals." Organizations and nations act as if they were made up only of parts, like the gears of a clock — big bosses, managers, workers, and so on.

Worldwork deals with more than the parts or parties. It is not a prescription for how people "should" behave. Such prescriptions always put down the opinions of minorities and people who are powerless. In conflict resolution and organizational development, the new paradigm creates rapid political and psychological change based on how people *actually* relate to one another.

The new paradigm assumes that people in groups are not necessarily dangerous or bad. They are capable of great wisdom and awareness. Instead of trying to control groups, worldwork helps people open up to one another, to the atmosphere.

ADDRESSING THE FIELD

Worldwork deals directly with the atmosphere of a group — its humidity, dryness, tensions and storms. This atmosphere, or "field," permeates us as individuals and spans entire groups, cities, organizations and the environment. The field can be felt; it is hostile or loving, repressed or fluid. It consists not only of such overt, visible, tangible structures as meeting agendas, party platforms and rational debate but also hidden, invisible, intangible emotional processes such as jealousy, prejudice, hurt and anger.

In any group, certain problems must be solved in a structured, linear, rational manner. These solutions will hold up, though, only if disturbances in the feeling atmosphere have been addressed first.

For instance, worldworkers are sometimes called on to solve city problems, ethnic conflicts, financial crises and crumbling corporate structures. The field is usually pervaded by desperation and hopelessness. If a worldworker sets out to remedy the situation using only legal measures or the application of sound fiscal practices, it would be like giving health food to people who are so depressed they want to die. Structural work is only a bandage unless feelings have been healed.

Sometimes the overall feeling atmosphere is so tense and depressed that people can't work on problems. A worldworker going into a failing business may call everyone together and question people about the atmosphere. What does it feel like? Who can express it? Are there people who can describe their feelings? The employees may be hopeless and full of anger at the bosses for denying them power. The bosses are afraid. When someone expresses this anger, the bosses' feelings change, and they relax. As a result, everyone becomes optimistic. They begin working together as a unit. The worldworker may not even have mentioned structural issues, but once the feeling problems have been addressed, the employees and bosses together can recreate their organization from scratch within a matter of hours.

(handwritten: sounds simplistic)

BRINGING UP HIDDEN MESSAGES

Employee hopelessness, which is common in failing businesses, provides an example of a message that is hidden in the field. The employees don't talk about it. They may be completely unaware of it. Yet it permeates the field and prevents anything constructive from happening.

Hidden messages are strong factors in the breakdown of group dynamics. These subtle and unexpressed attitudes, assumptions and dispositions may concern competition for leadership, hierarchical privileges, race relations, issues between women and men or older and younger people, environmental abuse, spiritual issues or private agendas at odds with the group's stated purpose. In fact, hidden messages can be generated around any kind of diversity. Diversity issues affect every organization, whether its purpose is to sell laundry detergent or to alleviate world hunger.

Often the organization's declared vision, structure and model are almost irrelevant compared to its ability to incorporate differences of opinion and diverse styles of communication. If a group succeeds at diversity, it is a successful community and will work. If it cannot do this, it fails at the deepest spiritual level of community, becomes unsustainable within itself and does little good for the world around it.

(handwritten: must be able to incorporate)

get-togethers, arguments at the local tavern, discussion circles, salons, lyceums and Chautauquas. They all bring people together to talk, learn and interact.

ALL THE WORLD'S PROBLEMS AT ONCE

One of the most common reasons why group negotiations break down is that so many people are afraid of anger. We can't or won't deal with hidden messages and agendas that involve aggression. Then feelings get submerged.

Repressed feelings, unfulfilled needs, the search for the meaning of life — all such human problems play central roles in every organization, regardless of its purpose or vision.

I have already named some of the social issues that arise out of diversity: use or misuse of hierarchical privilege, competition for power, race relations, relations between men and women or old and young, environmental abuse, and spiritual issues. We fan the flames by not admitting diversity exists.

The various levels of problems and issues are interwoven, so that solving any one of them without simultaneously addressing the others rarely works for long.

Your internal experiences, relationships and fate are connected with the economy, crime, drugs, racism and sexism, not only in your ethnic group and part of town, but also with other ethnic groups in other parts of town. It ends up that, whenever we work on one problem, we are working on the whole history of the human species. Because worldwork deals with the atmosphere and the field of a neighborhood, as well as with individuals and their roles in organizations, it doesn't work on problems linearly, one at a time. It takes on all the world's problems at once.

SOLUTIONS MAKE WAY FOR MORE PROBLEMS: A CASE IN POINT

I could give examples from Belfast or Moscow, Tel Aviv or Cape-town, Bombay, Tokyo or Odessa. Foremost in my mind right now is a tense conference in Compton, a low income section of Los Angeles that is battle-scarred from conflicts between Latino and Black gangs. This is an area whose problems the media sensationalizes and where residents are afraid to walk outside after dark.

DEMOCRACY: A PRIMITIVE FORM OF WORLDWORK

Worldwork during quiet times is easy, but in crisis the work becomes a fiery democratic procedure. Facilitators must bring forth and appreciate the views of those in power or in the mainstream, while dealing with the prejudices and hidden social, psychological and historical factors which create the experience of inequity.

Democracy is, really, a very basic but undeveloped form of worldwork. Democracy is to worldwork as a rowboat is to a sailboat. The rowboat requires human power; the sailboat moves *nature* with the wind. The Greek word *demokratia* means literally "people power."

Democracy functions through distribution or balance of power. But power is not something which can be balanced with rules. Democracy requires awareness. Without awareness of hidden signals, no one notices how many individuals and subgroups are marginalized and disenfranchised. Laws are meant to protect the rights of individuals and groups, but they are almost useless for dealing with subtle forms of prejudice and the way powerful people oppress others.

Worldwork not only punishes abuses of power, it brings power forward and makes it clear. Then it enables people to find their power and to create a fluid balance through interaction with others. Although the central social powers are economic class, race, religion, gender and age, there are many other powers that, once brought out, help create balance. I am thinking of the personal power of storytellers, elders, wise people and individuals with psychological centeredness, compassion and so forth, who change history through their presence. And I think of the power available to rebels, revolutionaries and terrorists, too.

Any power, good or bad, if not recognized, can become oppressive and hurtful. Hidden "mainstream" power, for example, lies behind the generally unexpressed assumption that oppressed people must dialogue politely to work out their problems, even though someone who feels oppressed usually does not want to speak gently. Such mainstream power is often hidden and unconscious. It operates pervasively in groups and can your fear, unhappiness or despair at being undervalued, you will stop thinking something is wrong with you and realize that you are doing something for all of us.

BRINGING OUT THE GHOSTS

Mainstream heterosexual couples have a lot of power. You realize this if you are single. Even when they enjoy being single, people may think there is something wrong with them for not being in a relationship, because society the world over gives rank to heterosexual relationships and not to singles.

People in lesbian, gay and bisexual relationships must endure enormous social deprecation. Heterosexuals have trouble imagining the pain involved in having a homosexual relationship. Gay men are frequently the target of "gay bashers," and must suffer the agony of watching their friends and lovers die of AIDS. Or they must suffer misunderstanding about AIDS, since some mainstream people think AIDS is a punishment for bad behavior. Lesbians endure the double-edged sword of homophobia and sexism. They are pressured to bear children and support traditional family values.

In addition to the harassment and religious, political and societal oppression homosexual couples suffer, in many communities it is expedient for them to hide their sexuality. Simply having most of the world believe there is something wrong, sick, perverted, abnormal, maladjusted, evil or infantile about you is a pressure difficult to combat. Sometimes you almost believe it yourself.

Many gay men, lesbians and bisexuals suffer from different forms of internalized oppression picked up from the mainstream. Homosexual relationships are burdened by some of the same issues that plague heterosexual relationships.

For example, there may be rank differences between partners if one is more "masculine" and the other more traditionally "feminine." The one with less experience or knowledge may feel inferior to the one with more experience or knowledge. Age, class, education and race are factors within all relationships.

When you bring into the open the hidden content of your face-to-face interactions, you are working on the world's issues. Your double signals contain all of them.

For instance, if you are in a heterosexual relationship, make use of your sexual orientation, knowing that it has the highest social rank. If you are unaware of your privileges, you ignore the problems of others and contribute to oppressing them. Use your heterosexual rank for your own benefit. Enjoy it! Express your affection publicly. Right there on the streets, give your partner a kiss. Make a speech about how everyone should be able to express love openly and how homosexuals cannot. Speak about how you have worked on your own homophobia. Ask people if they would be upset if you were a gay couple and you kissed publicly. Enter into debate.

Being heterosexual is not only a power but often a weakness as well. It can force you to relate only superficially to members of your own gender. Liberating your homosexual nature can mean freeing your interest and capacity to love everyone.

If you are in a racially homogeneous relationship, life is easier for you than for people in mixed race relationships. Enjoy your social privileges; show your affection, remembering that many racially mixed pairs cannot do this easily.

Have children or don't have them, but remember that your interests in family life are the same as those of some gays and lesbians who love kids. Use the privilege of having children, enjoy the kids, and then ask other parents whether homosexuals might not make very good parents, because suffering makes you more conscious of those who feel smallest.

Bring out the ghosts. Make community. I try to use my social rank as a white, middle-aged man in a heterosexual relationship by stirring up trouble while, at the same time, caring for individuals on all sides. I know my rank is relative. I realize that I owe most of my social consciousness to people who have less rank. My awareness would be lethargic without their provocation, advice and love.

THE PROCESS IS MYSTERY

Exploring power problems in relationships and groups, facilitators follow the unknown. They can never guess where the process will lead. Following the unknown is what sustainable community is nourished by.

A process is neither good nor bad, successful nor a failure, conservative nor liberal, masculine nor feminine. It is all of these things and none of them, because it is unpredictable and unknown. Where life is meant to go is unknown. Only the moment-by-moment signals of nature can be understood, not the larger purpose.

My own beliefs favor economic security for all and freedom from persecution and discrimination. But I also favor the overall process because it creates a community that is based on equality of awareness.

To follow process, you need a lot of strength and power, as well as consciousness of all your different ranks. Only then can you sense the mystery that has always been at the core of community, the realm of the unknown. Community process, like the world itself, is a strange, awesome experience, a place that is international and personal, intercultural, cultural and countercultural. Following the flow of communication, you go deeper and deeper into the mystery inside, between and among us.

True countercultural relationships are neither heterosexual, homosexual nor bisexual; they are neither good nor bad, masculine nor feminine. They neither support nor deny community. Countercultural relationships are constantly changing in content and form. Behind what seem to be impossible problems — projections, prejudice, racism, sexism and homophobia — is finally a path leading us, in an incomprehensible way, together.

Following the awareness of the spirit in everything sometimes seems, at first, to make trouble, even imprison us in prejudice. But in another moment it also liberates. It sometimes divides, but ultimately and suddenly unites in ways previously unimaginable.

Tolerate the moments of fear and chaos. Invite all the ghosts in. Try it. Bring your innerwork out, speak about your powers, use them to shine a light on prejudices, and discover what nature does next.

DISCOVER YOUR PRIVILEGES

The following questions are designed especially for people who are new to the topic of rank and privilege.

1. *What ethnic group do you belong to?* What ethnic group do others associate you with? What is your nationality? Gender? Profession?

Religion? Educational background? Economic class? Your relationship status? Age? Physical condition?

2. *What legal privileges or advantages do you feel deprived of because of
your identity?* What financial problems do you have that you feel
derive from your identity? What psychological problems do you
have that you feel are connected with your lack of social privilege?

3. *What privileges are connected with your identity?* Take time and be
specific. If you do not know, ask someone from another group to
tell you about your privileges.

Do you have travel/immigration privileges? Do you enjoy a
sense of belonging to a small community or to the majority? Do
you have intellectual, social or financial power? What privileges
are connected with being able-bodied and well? What are the
privileges of your gender? Speak about your sense of pride, your
earning capacity, your education, how your family is treated,
your age. Do others defer to your experience?

What do you own that's desirable to other people? What
privileges are connected to your choice of partner? With your
first language? With your education? Are you a good public
speaker? A confident leader?

4. *Celebrate your privileges in your mind or with friends.* Be grateful
for the luck you have, what pain your privileges spare you, how
they enrich your life. Be happy about them. Imagine, if you are
inclined, a divine being giving you these privileges. Ask that
divine being why you received these gifts.

If you cannot celebrate your privileges, consider the possibility that you have internalized the world's opinion about your
race, gender, or sexual orientation, making you prejudiced
against yourself. Or perhaps you can't celebrate because you
experience guilt for having something others don't.

5. *Remember your psychological privileges.* If you don't experience
problems coming from your childhood, you have rank others do
not have. Do you wake up in the morning looking forward to the
day? When you do, you have rank others don't enjoy. How often
do you feel centered and not anxious about the future? If frequently, you have a lot of psychological rank. What are your personal methods for working out tensions and problems? If they
succeed, you have a great deal of psychological rank.

6. *How about spiritual privileges?* Do you feel connected to your belief in life, or in life after death? Do you believe in a god? How does this connectedness influence your everyday life? Be thankful for whatever your privileges and connections are in this area. Heighten your consciousness by using them more. Speak about them. Celebrate them. Ask others how to share them.

7. *How are you using your most powerful privileges?* Choose one and ask how you use it at home, on the street, while shopping, at work, or in social groups. Think of several individuals or groups who do not have this privilege. Can you share or use your privileges to make others proud of theirs? To bring up problems and prejudice?

8. *What tensions and issues come up in your local group?* How are these tensions related to unconsciousness of your privileges?

9. *Imagine using your rank and privilege to change your relationship, your community, our world.*

5

Revenge & Cultural Transformation

DURING A TRIP TO BELFAST in 1992, I learned a lot about rank and how it gives rise to revenge and terrorism. I found out terrorists aren't tough guys, impervious to everything that's said to them. Instead they can be very sensitive. I learned that they are not "somewhere out there"; they exist in every group, as people who have been hurt by the mainstream and are fighting for everyone's freedom.

The conflict in Northern Ireland is between Catholics, who make up 43 percent of the population, and Protestants, who are 57 percent. The Catholic-backed Irish Republican Army (IRA) is the paramilitary wing of the Sinn Fein, the political movement whose name means literally "ourselves alone." The IRA and the Sinn Fein fight for a united Ireland free of British rule. The Protestant-loyalist population wants to remain attached to the lands of their ancestors, Scotland and England. The Protestants fear the loss of their cultural identity.

Since Amy and I were in Belfast, a cease fire has been agreed on, although at the time of this writing the IRA had not committed to working by peaceful means only. When we were there, Northern Ireland was 100 percent in conflict — unless you asked a resident.

People who live in conflict zones worldwide say that nothing special happens there. They have learned to dull their fears in order not to go crazy when bombings and killings are daily events. Belfast was an international metaphor for trouble spots in the world. It had been torn apart by conflict for decades.

All war zones are terrifying when you first enter them. Wherever you look, whether in Belfast or Beirut, people strain to get along as usual, numbing themselves to the omnipresent threat of snipers, bombs and terrorist attacks, which can happen anyplace, anytime, against anyone. Everyone here is shell-shocked, an example of what is called, in peaceful times, posttraumatic stress disorder.

Police stopped us repeatedly at the roadblocks where they were searching for terrorists. I hadn't had a gun pointed at me so many times since we had been in Israel in the 1980s.

Amy and I had been invited to the Belfast conference by a group made up of people from both sides of the conflict. Our meeting with these "terrorists" — a media word for people who identify themselves as freedom fighters — was held secretly. Participants knew they might be killed by their groups if their attendance was discovered. They were willing to risk their lives to find new ways of dealing with conflict. But, of course, practically everything during those times was a matter of life and death.

REVENGE CAN WAKE YOU UP

The conference got off to a rocky start. As Amy began her opening speech, one of the participants yelled in a belligerent tone, "Hey lady, what are ya waiting for? Tell us, already, if you know how to solve this bloody war, and don't take so long!"

Amy gave it back to him. "Be quiet, and let me have sixty seconds to talk."

The man and his friends continued to interrupt her. "I have been a terrorist for years," one of them bragged, as if challenging us to change him.

At first, we felt we were victims of an attack. A little reflection clarified things, however. The participants' anger was due in part to our having failed to acknowledge right away that they, the people living in this area, were the obvious experts on their own conflict.

It turned out that our lack of awareness of our privileges provoked them. We could go home and live in relative safety, but they had to stay there and live in a war zone. Our double signals — optimism about the potential good of conflict, dreams for a better world, messages of encouragement — made them feel like failures. Our mindless behavior aggravated their depression and infuriated them.

"An eye for an eye, a tooth for a tooth," one man said. They had to get back at us in order to wake us up. Before we could really talk with them, they had to make us suffer the conflict and agony they endured all the time. They succeeded; our enthusiasm temporarily disappeared.

This fight began in a split second but took two hours to settle. There seemed at first to be no content. The man and his friends were bitter and furious. This made us angry. The leader was especially nasty. Though he had been the one to set up the conference, he told us they had nothing to learn from us.

I became mean too, trying to gain vengeance like all the rest. I accused him of acting like a know-it-all dignitary. I told him he was a hopeless case and that he was preventing Northern Ireland from finding peace. He yelled that I was unfair to him and his friends.

One flurry led to the next, until a woman from their side intervened. She explained to us that the man who seemed the most belligerent was simply being himself. "He doesn't intend to be nasty," she said. "He thinks he is doing something good for everybody!" As she soothed us, our attacker fell quiet.

She was right. I had assumed that he identified with being tough and vengeful, but she got him to demonstrate that this was not the case. Thanks to that insightful woman, we resolved the fight and went on to have a good meeting. We worked on the desire for vengeance and the hope for transformation. In the end, the "terrorist" who had attacked Amy invited us to the neighborhood pub.

Anytime we, as facilitators, suggest that we know something others do not, we act like teachers set over everyone else. The formula is simple: the unconscious use of rank causes revenge.

I could have avoided the whole problem by noticing my rank. My opponent could have, too. On the other hand, we needed our mutual vengefulness to become aware of rank. In our unconsciousness, he meant to do something good, and so did I.

That evening, I learned that terrorism is not just a political activity, but a frequent and unseen group interaction based upon the sense of being treated unjustly. Everyone gets angry at one time or another. Most of us know what it means to seek revenge for hurts inflicted on us. After all, much of childhood is about growing to protect ourselves from wounds inflicted by those who use their power unconsciously. Nevertheless, psychologists have just begun to understand shame and abuse; group and political facilitators know little or nothing about them. That is why we tell those who are furious and full of vengefulness that they must work on themselves, as if they alone created the problem. Our newspapers are full of misunderstandings of those who are furious. Our legal system is overburdened with cases in which revenge was the motive, because the system deals with anger and terrorism as if it occurred out of the clear blue sky, independently of mainstream behavior.

The problem is pandemic. Every few seconds someone is raped, robbed or murdered in the United States. Poverty, drugs, joblessness, lack of education, racism, sexism and social abuse promote violence. That social injustice foments revenge should be obvious from the fact that the vast majority of those incarcerated for violent acts in all countries come from the groups with the fewest social privileges. In other words, violence occurs, in part, because the oppressed cannot defend themselves from the intentional and covert use of mainstream rank.

Revenge is a form of spirituality, a sort of spiritual power meant to equalize social injustice. In the Bible, it is God who recommends an eye for an eye in Leviticus 24:20, "When one man injures and disfigures his fellow-countryman, it shall be done to him as he has done; fracture for fracture, eye for eye, tooth for tooth; the injury and disfigurement that he has inflicted upon another shall in turn be inflicted upon him." There are many

l the fundamentalist group were terrified of being
ther and wanted an end to hostilities.

hot spots had an amazing effect on that open
rd, some of the speakers for the fundamentalist
that they had not realized how much the gays
One of the gay group said he was unaware of the
ents had suffered.

BEYOND REVENGE IN MOSCOW

eeting set up by members of the ex-Soviet Peace
r delving into vengeance produced unexpected
seemingly impossible conflicts. The gathering
hundred and fifty people, government officials
tries of the former Soviet Union as well as teachers,
and political scientists from all over the world.
rmally dressed — men in ties, women in hats. They
en us before and had been sent as delegates from
s to experiment for five days with new methods of
d conflict resolution.

sphere was tense. Many of the Russian delegates
oups that had engaged in bloody battles since they
eased from domination by Soviet authority. After
of discussion about these battles, Amy and I asked
m the countries of the Caucasus mountain range to
in the center of the group, to deepen our focus on
s. They represented peoples who had been fighting
, in some cases for centuries.

ber of the Georgian parliament announced that this
ric occasion: the first time people from Azerbaijan,
orgia, Abkhazia, Ossetia, Ingustia and Russia had
r to work on things collectively. His optimism pro-
mer of hope in the midst of the depression and
e inadequately heated room.

the positive feeling was downed by the harshness of
m outside the circle. Some of these people had been
the Soviet Secret Police (KGB). Their behavior
lty; they didn't care what anyone else might do or
hey spoke, we felt chills run through our bodies.
ers seemed terrified of the ex-KGB officers.

beautiful quotes from God in the Bible, but the divine penchant for vengeance is there, too.

Vengeance is central to religious teachings. Confucius tried to compensate for it by advising, "What you do not want done to yourself, do not do to others." Christ taught, "Do unto others as you would have them do unto you." Buddhists cultivate loving kindness. Nevertheless, when we seek revenge, we are apt to feel we have some sort of divine justification for our actions. This felt sense of "justice" transmutes chronic violence into a sort of religious struggle against "evil-doers." Since we have been hurt, we feel we have a right to get back at our persecutors. Abused people have only two choices: either they go numb or they become abusers themselves.

PASSIVITY: THE FIRST SIGN OF REVENGE

Revenge begins with repressed anger. Some of us just grind our teeth and smile when we have been hurt. From such beginnings, the urge for revenge can grow until it instigates revolution.

Vengefulness is a double signal when you restrain yourself because you are afraid of being hurt by someone more powerful than you. To protect yourself from retaliation, you dissociate from your rage and try to act as if it's not there.

Repressing anger may be the wisest thing to do. In some parts of the world, the price of revenge against someone with higher social rank is torture, imprisonment or death. In every country, children defending themselves against an abusive parent run the risk of greater harm.

Ironically, the first signal of desire for revenge may be passivity: shock, shame, numbness, withdrawal or anxiety. It is important to notice these early signs, because they inevitably activate the cycle of the talionic impulse: revenge for revenge.

In its early stages, the desire for revenge manifests in sometimes subtle forms: foot-dragging, coming to work late, avoiding a conversation, being absent-minded, going on strike, not reacting when spoken to, storming out, despair or weeping. Depression and bad moods can be ways of getting back at others or making them feel guilty.

Later, the desire for revenge is manifest in the formation of coalitions opposed to the oppressors. Eventually, revenge is

sought in demonstrations against authorities, riots, civil disobedience and finally revolution.

COMMUNITY THROUGH LOVE OR HATE

As I have stressed before, revenge would not be necessary if we
were all wiser about our rank and more conscious of our use of
social power. Revenge itself is an uncanny power that the privileged are unable to defend against.

It happens again and again — between bosses and workers,
parents and children, authorities and the disenfranchised, afflu-
ent countries and those that are poor. When we are oblivious to
being one-up on others, we are rudely awakened by someone
with less rank.

Privileged people say that community is created through loving one another, through sharing food and doing things together.
Many of the disenfranchised have another story to tell. For them,
community begins with bathing the world in hatred. Their pain
escalates to dissent, invective and finally violence and revenge.

The people who are the objects of this revenge experience
themselves as innocent victims, further infuriating the disenfranchised. Yet revenge is their only means of getting attention for the
injustice they suffer. Without this fury, the rest of the world
would never have to face its abuses of power. People who are
powerless see it this way: the less conscious we are of our power,
the less we care about their concerns.

Our "justice" system is simply another form of unconsciousness. Standard practice in criminology and psychopathology
assumes that acts of revenge are due to the "criminal's" personal
history. I suggest changing this practice and viewing antisocial
behavior as due to the social context in which it takes place. We
could reduce "criminal" behavior by spending some of the
money spent on prisons to advance education about rank.

HANDLING HOT SPOTS

As I explained in Chapter One, a hot spot is an emotional, angry,
surprising or frozen moment in a group meeting. Hot spots are
whirling vortices of energy that escalate and sweep like a tornado
over everyone in their path, resulting even in riots and violence.

Hot spots involvin
nals of rank. Consider
man who held his Bib
needed help. A man fr
wanted to throw a bric
homosexuals. The man

This was a hot spot.
condescending smile. It
the objects of it respond
counter-threat from the
away, or else!" His do
behavior shows how stuj

Notice the symmetry
insult provokes insult. Sy
counter-threats are seriou
chain reaction of more t
may follow.

A good facilitator reli
it, exploring threats and
fury? Say more. Is it due t
is behind your smile? Do y
your help?" What elders o
as their intent to promote

There are several choic
hot spot and letting the fl
simply recreate the hurtful
one party for an extended
shamed.

I suggest dealing briefly
time, making sure everyone
heard. This might mean ask
desire for revenge provoked
A question to the smiling n
forth a moral code a compen
control of themselves and hu

I have posed these ques
tions. In one town meeting,
his incredibly painful childl
world was getting out of han
munity spoke of similar issu
discovered something they ha

community an
hurt by one an
Exploring
forum. Afterw
group told me
were suffering
pain his oppon

In 1990, at a
Committee, o
solutions to
included one
from the coun
psychologists
They came fo
had never se
their countrie
democracy ar

The atmo
came from gr
had been rel
several hours
delegates fro
form a circle
their problen
over territory

One me
was an histo
Armenia, G
come togeth
vided a glir
despair in th

But soo
speakers fro
members o
exuded cru
say. When
Other speak

Amy and I doubted that anything positive would emerge from the people in the circle. Some of them said they had come to the conference to attract Western attention for ethnic causes in their countries; they didn't want to negotiate with other countries of the Caucasus for the resolution of mutual problems. They blatantly or indirectly expressed their dislike for their opponents and wanted the West to intervene.

Other delegates had never attended such a large open forum, since only small groups had been allowed to assemble in the former Soviet Union. They reverted to what they knew and decided to hold forth with official sounding speeches.

To break the tension, we invited the twenty delegates from the Caucasian mountain range to sit on the floor.

THE GHOSTS APPEAR

Like most people accustomed to discussing matters at a table or meeting over drinks, they were shy at first about sitting on the floor. But soon they began to speak from the heart.

Amy and I were touched by what we heard. We listened for timespirits and hidden agendas. After there had been plenty of opportunity for everyone to speak, we pointed out that people had directly or indirectly mentioned several ghost roles, that is, aspects of the group's process that were not represented by anyone.

One of the ghosts present was the Terrorist. People spoke of violent freedom fighters from smaller countries who risked their lives for revenge against Russia for previous injuries and present resistance to independence.

The Dictator was also among us. Delegates criticized the central, imperialist Soviet rulers who "wanted to dominate other countries."

The Facilitator was trying to manifest. Some delegates were trying to negotiate peace.

We suggested making these ghost roles visible by playing them. At first, most of the delegates were reluctant to take a role other than what they believed to be their true selves. They said the whole situation was too serious and made them uneasy. To our surprise, however, some participants tried our suggestion. Soon they divided into three groups, playing the three roles. We suggested that people join one of the three groups representing the role they felt closest to at the moment. We also recommended that they switch roles, moving whenever their feelings shifted.

On one side of the room people stood for the Dictator. Against the opposite wall were both the Terrorist and Facilitator.

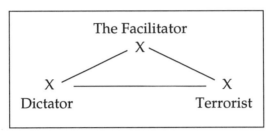

Timespirits in the Field

People were allowed to speak all at once if they chose. At first, the process of free, open dialogue stymied them. They were used to a lecture style of communication, where one person spoke and those who were bored left the room or read newspapers.

The new style succeeded in breaking through. It transformed politeness and decorum into a chilling dialogue between the Central Committee and the Terrorist, who threatened to blow up bridges and otherwise get revenge. The Central Committee counter-threatened, "If you try, that will be the end of all of you."

Suddenly everything changed. A Georgian delegate left the Terrorist position, moved quickly across the room, and became the Communist Party Boss from Moscow. He yelled that everyone must follow the dictates of the Soviet Central Committee. Somehow, hearing him express the power and rank from that position, people felt better. It was a relief to have rank expressed clearly; then at least people knew what they were fighting against. Otherwise, the Dictator was a spirit who could not quite be caught.

Now there was a lot of movement in the room. More delegates joined the Terrorist. They taunted and threatened the Party Boss, something they would not have dared to do, even as play-acting, just a year or two earlier. Those trying to facilitate were paralyzed in the background as the inner circle made transitions from serious political discussion to threats, to stalemate, and finally to hilarious play.

The people acting out the Dictator became so stubborn, arrogant and privileged that, to gain revenge, the Terrorists had to lift the actors into the air and carry them away from their positions. Everyone burst out laughing. The Dictator seemed impotent, flailing about on the shoulders of the Terrorist. The onlookers were so excited that they could hardly wait for their Russian words to be translated into other languages. Though Amy and I understood little Russian, we could easily follow the process that had been unleashed.

FROM TIMESPIRITS TO RESOLUTIONS

The group discovered a resolution as the actors, now engaged in generating ideas beyond their drama, created a new role, the Starving Citizen.

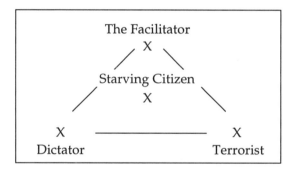

Timespirits in the Field

One delegate acted out a desperate scene of starvation, lying on the floor, wailing and waiting for death. The people who had been the Terrorists nursed and fed this starving person.

Suddenly the exercise was over. After forty-five minutes, it ended as rapidly as it had begun.

Everyone — including those Muscovites with the greatest rank — understood that they had lost touch with their common problem: people's suffering and marginalization. Through the exercise, they remembered the pain and suffering that were their common motivation to work together.

Many participants were deeply touched not only by the resolution, but by the ability of the large group to get beyond power and vengefulness. People seemed ready to devise solutions to the needs of the mainstream and the marginalized alike. In the three days that followed, they created an organization called *If Not We, Then Who?*, which is headquartered in Moscow. The delegates also formulated a statement about peace, freedom and negotiation. The statement was later signed by Edward Shevardnadze, President of Georgia and former foreign minister of the USSR.

The group had broken through an apparently hopeless impasse — every country for itself — when, in the aftermath of play-acting as vengeful terrorists, they had an emotional realization that they all wanted to relieve suffering. Community occurs even during ethnic and ancient conflict when the power of the mainstream and the wisdom of terrorists connect. Previously unheard-of solutions are created.

There are no permanent solutions to social problems. It is necessary to come together again and again, notice the timespirits and express their intentions. The community we find in this way is more sustainable than temporary solutions to problems.

THE VENGEFULNESS BEHIND FOREIGN POLICY

Though we are aware of vengefulness in our personal lives, we scarcely notice that our international policies can also be based on a desire for revenge. The United States punishes other countries. For example, when the CIA learned of an Iraqi plot — which had not been carried out — to kill President Bush, the United States bombed Iraq. An enlightened U.S. could instead have invited representatives of the Iraqis to do a TV program in which both countries processed their belligerence against one another. If whole nations could see proceedings such as Amy and I witnessed in Moscow, new solutions to world problems might evolve.

At present, unprocessed vengefulness is globally accepted as the driving force of foreign policy. German aggression against Poland that signaled World War II was greeted with complacency in other countries. After all, Germany was revenging itself for the humiliating loss of territory in the Treaty of Versailles at the end of World War I. Jews by the millions were the victims of German revenge for the economic sanctions of the Treaty of Versailles. In their turn, Israelis have dealt harshly with Palestinians.

Revenge is also the "modus operandi" of many individuals. Whether we are in business, church groups, a philosophy seminar, the community police force, bowling team, city council, street gang, or simply the family, there are bound to be individuals with a hidden agenda of gaining revenge for recognition not received in the past.

Love and hope draw us together. Economics, politics and spirituality may inspire us. But the fear of being publicly hurt by angry, vengeful comments or terrorized by subtle oppression restrains our participation in meetings and depresses progressive movements. Power battles and hidden vengeance pollute group and international life more than toxic fumes. We can expect riots in our cities and murders in the suburbs as long as minority issues are ignored.

Violence will stop only when you and I are ready to work on it. That entails interrupting our lives to include awareness of the agony of the oppressed.

When we work on vengefulness, we are in the most ancient and yet the newest undiscovered territory. I thought I had finished with my own vengefulness until I began working with large groups. I thought I knew myself, but I found myself losing my temper out of desire to gain revenge, not only for what was happening to others in my adult world at that moment, but also for what had happened to me in childhood.

It was a Black South African woman from Capetown who revealed to me that I had forgotten my own urge for revenge. During a discussion about conflict between Bantus and Zulus, she stood up and screamed that if the other side did not get its act together, she would kill them after our meeting.

A white South African woman, shocked by her outburst, said, "Surely you do not want to kill! After all, killing is a sin."

The Black woman slowly turned and faced the white woman. In a compassionate yet powerful voice, she explained, "Listen, honey, you don't realize what a relief it would be to kill!"

In a flash, I realized I was like that white woman. I had been fooling myself into thinking that everyone should outgrow hatred, vengefulness and jealousy. I have changed now. Today I know that the fury behind revenge is just the beginning of an important process. It is one of the many forces that can launch cultural transformation.

AWARENESS TRAINING IN VENGEFULNESS

Worldworkers who want to feel, notice and deal with vengeful-ness in others need to work on their own tendencies toward retal-iation. Here are questions to help you reflect on your own desire for vengeance:

1. Recall a long-standing conflict you had with another person or group. Can you remember being upset, angry, even wanting revenge?

2. What role did other people's conscious or unconscious use of social, psychological or spiritual rank play in your desire to retal-iate? What kind of rank did they have? How did they use it? How was their rank hidden and difficult to defend against? Did they behave like dictators or totalitarians?

3. Did you want to harm the others physically or psychologi-cally? Did you gossip about them and put them down? Do you think your revenge was provoked only by them or also by past abuse you were unable to defend yourself against?

4. Consider whether your desire for revenge prolonged the con-flict.

5. Imagine that the conflict you are recalling is beginning again today. Imagine having the courage to notice your own and the other's rank, spending more time embracing your vengefulness, and getting beyond it by getting into it.

6

Embracing The Terrorist

EVERYONE IS AFRAID OF GHOSTS. A ghost role in a group is something we feel but cannot see. Repressed vengeance leads to terrorism, and the terrorist makes everyone anxious. This role is filled by most of us at one time or another because just about everyone wants revenge for past abuses. The terrorist fights for freedom and justice against another role, the role of social power and collective domination. Thus, the terrorist is a potential ghost role in any group, anywhere, at any time.

Like governments, organizations try to repress terrorists. *Robert's Rules of Order*, organizational development techniques and rewards for those who say yes to management are methods of keeping the terrorist down. Governments everywhere fear the future because of repressed rage and terrorism. Just as no one person or group is the mainstream, so no one person or group is the terrorist. We all find ourselves sometimes in the place of power and other times trying to gain vengeance against the abuse of power.

Terrorism is a spirit of the times when there is need of cultural change but it is blocked. The terrorist becomes a ghost role. We don't yet consciously notice terrorism, but we feel it and create institutions to keep it down. Our efforts at repressing revenge have made the terrorist an unhappy ghost lurking behind the scenes in our everyday life.

Politicians and sociologists alike have trouble defining terrorism because they share the mainstream's concepts of violence and the use of illegal force. For example, the specialists represented in *Violence, Terrorism and Justice,* edited by R. G. Frey and C. W. Morris, more or less agree that terrorism is an organized political act of intentional killing.

What does "organized" mean? Who decides when something becomes intentional? What killing is not a political act? I prefer to reserve the concept of terrorism for groups and individuals fighting against mainstream power from socially marginal, minority or disenfranchised positions — freedom fighters, as I said in the last chapter.

Super powers such as the United States cannot be terrorists. Intentional killing by a nation of privilege that is not at war, I call "imperialism." Political interventions like those by the United States against Libya, Nicaragua and Iraq, in which the U.S. bombed or destroyed other groups by supporting paramilitary forces, were imperialistic, even though they were either denied or characterized in official statements as necessary to the "national interest." Powerful countries portray themselves as victims of terrorism. In this way imperialism becomes a ghost.

Howard Zinn, in *People's History of the United States,* points out that the Monroe Doctrine of 1823 claimed the Western Hemisphere as a possession of the United States. The United States intervened twenty times in the Caribbean between 1900 and 1933 so that U.S. banking, mining and fruit companies could move in. Millions of acres of land used by the indigenous people for food were appropriated for commercial crops such as bananas, coffee, cocoa and pineapple.

Imperialism is the overt or hidden policy of national, territorial or economic expansion supported by government attacks and coupled with the passivity of that nation's mainstream citizens.

When imperialism is hidden, it is doubly abusive, since people cannot protect themselves against what cannot be seen.

Terrorism is different. It is characterized by disempowered groups' attacks on the mainstream for the sake of equality and freedom. What appears as random and unjustified violence to the mainstream is actually freedom fighters' attempts to compensate for the hurts they have suffered. Their goal is to awaken those in power to the necessity of social change. From the terrorists' viewpoint, no mainstream person they injure or kill is an innocent victim. Every mainstream person participates, if only passively, in the oppression terrorists fight against.

My definition of terrorism also includes revenge by means of group processes that cause psychological pain or damage. The threat of violence falls into this category, as do exposures of culpability. We experience such terrorism often. Perhaps the woman in a heterosexual relationship says to her partner, "Either be more sensitive to my needs or I'm gone." He experiences this as terrorism; at any moment, she may pull the rug out from under their relationship. But she feels that her needs are so unimportant to him that nothing less than destroying the relationship will cause sufficient awakening.

Terrorism is not an isolated, international incident involving a stolen airplane. Terrorism is as common as people getting together. Whenever someone says in a group, "Either you do this or I am walking out," the entire group is held at gunpoint, so to speak. The problem of terrorism cannot be solved at the international level alone. It must be dealt with at the grass roots level, in the family, the school, the church, local organizations and local government.

This expands the definition of terrorism to include, not only marginalized groups enacting politically motivated revenge, but also relationship and group processes that cause fear or psychological pain. Terrorism is a social process that ranges from small-scale to international; it is engaged in by disempowered individuals or groups taking revenge for past and current use of rank, intentionally or unconsciously, and hoping to establish equality.

DE-PATHOLOGIZING TERRORISM

Some therapists categorize an inclination toward terrorism as a "narcissistic disorder." Rebellion is often seen as evidence of "paranoia." By diagnosing terrorist behavior as inappropriate, deviant, sociopathic or psychopathic, psychology and psychiatry lull the mainstream into deeper complacency. They imply that there's nothing wrong with the political or social status quo; the problems are internal to the troublemakers.

Therapists must realize the social implications of categorizing violent reactions as "inappropriate." Diagnoses based upon mainstream cultural assumptions may be racist or sexist and abuse power, prestige, safety and privilege. As long as psychiatry and psychology are socially unaware, they will put down youth, women, the poor, People of Color, older people, gays and lesbians, "criminals" and people suffering from substance abuse, as if all of these people should solve their problems without the rest of the world's having to change. In this way, psychology exacerbates problems instead of alleviating them.

Fortunately, some voices have been raised against mainstream attitudes toward marginalized behavior. Feminist psychologist Phyllis Chessler, in *Women and Madness*, attacks psychiatric diagnoses, treatment and suppression of women. Alice Miller's work has indicted psychoanalysis for helping perpetuate childhood abuse by denying it. Jeffrey Masson, who was fired as director of the Freud Archives, has described Freud's "cover up" of his initial hypothesis that women patients actually had been sexually abused as children. Reich, Moreno and Adler were all aware of the social implications of labeling behavior neurotic or psychotic.

Insisting that psychological work take precedence over social change is abusive and undemocratic. The terrorist arises in us all when we feel unheard or unable to protect ourselves from oppressive situations created by people and groups that are too big, powerful or awesome for an individual to fight "fairly."

So-called "pathological, borderline, dysfunctional, or psychotic" people who disturb or threaten the mainstream are potential world-changers. We need to find value and not just the pathology in symptoms. Inner experiences are important for culture. Certainly, they sometimes shock the mainstream. Yet visions are transformative. I hope that de-pathologizing terrorism will enable us to see it as a common social process with the potential to help create a more equitable world.

TERRORISM HAS CHANGED YOUR LIFE

Terrorism polarizes groups. The terrorist's intention is to highlight divisions a group may not recognize. As a facilitator, it has helped me to remember this. Terrorists want to make the mainstream assume responsibility for social change. They aim to make it impossible for anyone to escape social consciousness by reminding us that the world is a theater in which each of us acts a particular role, whether we like it or not. Even if we are only standing by watching, passivity implies acceptance of the status quo. Terrorists are hurt by our negativity, aloofness and disinterest, even if they can't see, hear, or touch these attitudes.

Likewise, we are hurt by the terrorist's hidden negativity. We feel hidden messages even if we do not see or hear them. That is what makes us afraid of people and situations without knowing why. We feel anger but can't "put our finger on it."

Remember a time when you had to lead a group, teach or give a speech and felt that someone in the audience was against you. How did that affect your performance? If it was your first teaching experience, for instance, you might have decided not to become a teacher. Terrorism has influenced your life, perhaps more than you realize.

You can defend yourself against intended negative messages, because they are direct. You hear and see the points the others are making. But hidden ones are more difficult to detect and decipher, and you must follow your feelings. If terrorists spoke directly, those who have rank would punish them. Social power, in the experience of terrorists, limits freedom, represses communication and makes it dangerous to speak openly.

Before the downfall of the Soviet Union, people in Poland could not, with safety, speak out against the government. They could only hum in unison as they sat in the trains like proper citizens. The police could not see who was humming. People resort to double signals when there is no hope of direct communication. The terrorist must resort to hidden methods, and you as a mainstream person must sometimes resort to depending on your feelings or an awareness of double signals to know the terrorist is present.

GHOSTS AT WAR

Democratic countries always take the position that everyone is equal, yet they shun terrorists and ignore issues of hopelessness, depression and fury. The hidden signals of those in power imply, "I don't want to hear from you. You and your difficulties are not important. Stay away from me with your problems."

Facilitators must be quick to recognize such marginalizing signals, gestures and behavior, because conflicts cannot be resolved until unconscious behavior is brought to awareness. The facilitator must acknowledge the war between ghosts. Others may not see it, but it poisons the atmosphere and makes everyone afraid. The mainstream ghost says, "Sit down and be quiet. Who invited you here, anyway? You are inappropriate."

The marginalized ghost answers, "Wake up! You are on trial! If you don't listen to us, we'll put a bomb in your home. *That* should wake you up."

Since those in power rarely notice when and how they put others down, they experience "terrorist" attacks as unfair, coming from those they least suspected, occurring in surprising places and times, and using secret, unnecessarily hurtful or violent tactics.

Amy and I were surprised by our attacker in Belfast. We thought of him only as a seminar participant. He experienced himself as having to fight for recognition. We had inadvertently conveyed the impression that we thought he did not know enough about conflict resolution. Neither side understood the signals and messages of the other. We felt that he was not following the rules of etiquette: be gracious to your guest and do not interrupt while she is speaking. According to us, it would have been more appropriate for him to have waited to speak and then not to have been nasty or unnecessarily vehement.

Those of us who have the privilege of living outside a conflict zone create terrorism by thinking people are crazy in places like Belfast. Newspaper readers around the world shake their heads in disbelief: "How can those people continue to kill one another? We would not do that." "We" become the mainstream ghost, living in safety, projecting our own hurtful nature onto others while punishing them for being belligerent.

We have this condescending attitude because we are not conscious of our own terrorism. Resolving violence and terrorism requires every level of organization, from the individual to the United Nations, not only to tolerate but also to understand the rage, hurt and need for transformation. In my view, the smaller arenas are as important as the world at large. World problems must be addressed in local forums where we can storm, be furious and still be heard.

The most fundamental forum is your own heart. Both as a facilitator and as a human being, you must learn to hear yourself there. Then you will know how to hear others when they are angry and hurt. The less we listen, the angrier people become, not only because of their enemies, but because of us. If we will hear the terrorist speak — even though we are not personally in much of a position to help alter the social problem — we begin implementing the solution: deep democracy.

LIKE RANK, TERRORISM CAN BE A DRUG

Once people experience the power of revenge to create dissent and change the world, terrorism can be addictive. In German, revenge is called *die Rachsucht*, which translated literally means "addiction to fury." Righteous power feels good. It's "sweet" and provides a rush of satisfaction. Sometimes you can't get enough.

It is a quick step from getting back at an individual for a specific wrong to getting back at everybody for everything. That is how terrorists go too far and become the problem they set out to fight against: they too are guilty of the unconscious abuse of power.

Social activists know this well. Mary E. Gomes reported in "The Rewards and Stresses of Social Change: A Qualitative Study of Activists"[1] that, among peace activists, stresses within the movement included infighting, factionalism, personality conflicts, an intolerant atmosphere, domineering individuals, power-hunger, sexism, racism and frustrating delays caused by narcissistic speakers.

It should really be no surprise that those of us who are driven to correct the wrongs in culture can be overbearing, intolerant, and ready for factionalism and infighting. We are all burdened by internal domination. Wanting change in the world drives us to use all sorts of power. A victim of anti-semitism can be a racist. A victim of racism may be homophobic. Some victims of homophobia

are sexist. Any of us can be the victim of one process and simultaneously a perpetrator of another. In warning others not to abuse
power, we are heard best when we remain aware that our own
use of power can be blind and addictive.

As a worldworker, you must not abuse your power by asking
others to change to make your job easier. People are needed by
the world just as they are. You can change your attitude by artic-
ulating their views as spirits in the field.

Notice these characteristics of terrorism in group processes:

1. *Needing Power.* Feeling that you don't have enough power,
you use methods that those who do have power cannot easily defend against, including double signals. You gossip
against them in the background of group discussions or burst
forth into the midst of meetings to disrupt the governing system. If possible, you would hold a whole group hostage to
get your way.

2. *Despair.* You suffer from despair because you have given
up on working gradually for change from the inside. You feel
you are up against overpowering odds. Your emotions are
violent, though you may look cool.

3. *Recklessness.* You work for the highest ideals and will go up
against anyone who steps in your way. You break accepted
rules of safety in communication in order to force the power
group to hear your unpopular opinions. In fact, you will even
risk your life to make your point. You want to make the
world as unsafe for others as it is for you.

4. *Allegiance.* Your vengefulness runs so deep that it extends
to the people with whom you identify. You condemn what
has been done to you, your race, gender, religion, family, culture and civilization. Your rage is both current and ancient; it
goes back to your groups' basic roots.

5. *Addiction.* You constantly seek confrontation with an
authority figure. Your righteousness is not bound by a local-
ity or a field or one particular kind of abuse. It attacks the
authorities of any group. You need an enemy at all times. If

no authority figure is available, you imagine your peers to be your opponents and attack them.

6. *Injunction against Retaliation.* Your attack may begin something like, "It is difficult to say this in the group, because I fear reprisals from anyone here who is prejudiced, but I feel I must speak out." You cast yourself as a courageous hero. Anyone who counterattacks has already been labeled prejudiced. In this way, you forestall discussion, debate and retaliation.

7. *Condemnation of the Group.* Another message that's difficult to defend against is the ultimatum: "I am going to leave this group because you people are not changing. As far as I'm concerned, you're as bad as the rest of them, and I am personally going to make sure you get something you cannot defend against."

8. *Self-destruction.* Your grief is so vast and your hatred so uncontainable that you injure those you need the most. Terrorism can become so strong that it chases away just those people who might be useful to the cause. Your hatred even injures those you love, including yourself.

9. *Unconsciousness of Strength.* As a terrorist, you have a kind of spiritual rank. You may not identify with this power or be aware of it. Remember the terrorist in Belfast who attacked Amy? Afterward, when we became friends, he confided to us that he had not realized how powerful he was or that he was being hurtful. He did not think he was sabotaging the group atmosphere. He hadn't been aware of wanting to get back at us for the life he led, scarcely above the poverty line. He had thought his life had been weak and not sufficiently effectual. But he was righteously motivated to rectify injustices from the past.

TERRORISTS CAN CHANGE

In spite of this formidable list of terrorism's characteristics, terrorists are just people. They are neither insane nor psychotic. Whether they come from North Korea, Basqueland, the West Bank of Israel, the United States, Germany, Central or South America, women and men tell stories about their families who have been so injured that honor demands retaliation. For a moving book on this subject, read Eileen McDonald's, *Shoot the Women First*, an incredible investigation of the power of women.

People who have become addicted to violence as a means of correcting injustices are more flexible than the media would allow us to believe. They can change rapidly. Everyone can potentially change — even those who block awareness of their mainstream power. Wherever there are people, change remains possible.

A Belfast man told the seminar participants how he had become a terrorist. When he was a boy, he saw two British secret service agents shoot his father in the head. He went with his father in the ambulance to the hospital. His father leaned towards him and whispered, "Forgive the killers."

But he couldn't. All he wanted was to retaliate for his father's murder. He swore to devote his life to seeking revenge. He joined a terrorist group.

A priest in our group was amazed and shocked to hear such vengefulness. After discussing the situation, the priest opened up to the other man's desire for revenge. As the priest changed, suspending his own judgments, he became compassionate towards the terrorist. Then the terrorist changed, too. He admitted he did not want to kill anymore. He would be happier teaching kids how to resolve problems in other ways. We all sat there astonished. The fluidity and generosity of the priest had enabled the transition.

Ron, another terrorist, had been beaten, shot and almost killed by terrorists. He told us that he had joined the Protestant army when his friends were killed. His commander told him to kill one of the leaders on the other side. He stalked the man for months. When he finally met him on the street, Ron shot the man down. As his victim lay on the ground, he continued shooting him in the legs, again and again.

For three years, Ron sat behind bars plotting the death of an informer who had turned him in. But then, by some ironic twist of fate, the informer became one of his jailers, a prison guard who walked in front of his cell every day. Ron told us about one special moment, sitting in the midst of his fury in that cell, when he realized that everyone in his family would be killed if he did not stop this cycle of murder. That sudden realization changed him. When he got out of jail, instead of taking revenge against the informer, he left terrorism behind. Now he works for the resolution of conflict. That's why he came to our meeting.

People can transform themselves spontaneously and go on to help the world in sustainable ways. Having tried, at one point or another, to arrive at our goals through force, most of us switch to nonviolent methods.

SITTING IN THE FIRE

Your group, indeed our whole world, stands or falls depending upon how you and the rest of us deal with terrorism in ourselves and others. As you facilitate, you have an opportunity to model coping with violent tension. You are perceived as an authority and you are vulnerable to attack. Can you embrace the terrorist? It's not easy, but if you remember your own freedom fights, it's also not hard.

During one conference, a white woman accused me of ignoring her raised hand. In a powerful voice that scared me, she said that I was using my position against her. I was hurt by her but admired the courage she showed in confronting me.

When we sat in the center, I told her that I had not seen her raised hand, but I nevertheless understood how she felt. I indeed had powers that could be used against her. She responded that she was fed up with the Black-white issues the group was focused on. They did not relate to her. She wanted to change the subject of discussion. I said I understood that she felt marginalized by the group's focus, but I also felt very sad. I decided to follow my feelings.

I said that, although I was one of the main facilitators and had a great deal of power in the moment, I felt impotent against her. Outside that particular meeting place, her viewpoint had all the power in the world. I told her that I felt she was therefore more powerful than I. Racism was a terribly important subject to me, and all I could do was weep at my inability to get others to take it as seriously as I did.

She changed on the spot. She understood what I was trying to say, and she said she felt heard. She turned out to be a courageous and insightful woman. She helped me go deeper into myself, told me that I needed help and gave it to me by listening. Then we went on to her issues. Her anger about my having ignored her raised hand helped connect us. Attack, revenge and terrorism were only a first stage in the relationship. We spoke together at length later. My first impression had been that she was a very powerful person; I had both respected and feared her. Now I found her to be a fine teacher with a lot of great ideas about social change. I could discover this only by sitting in the fire.

The basic goals of socially marginalized people who resort to violence are "bread" (gaining economic support), freedom and the respect necessary to survive. Calling them "terrorists" is useless. It is up to you as a facilitator to understand and help them express the message behind their attack — help them talk about peace, justice and bread. You can help change their appearance as "enemies" to "allies."

Imagine students who are troublesome and cannot quite explain why. Imagine addressing terrorists who are not clearly identified with their anger or social position. It is important to say that you are guessing that they are fighting for the best interests of a disempowered group such as women, Blacks or youth. Suppose that, as a facilitator, you want to discover or support them so that their issues can be dealt with openly. One way to do this is to ask for permission to speak for the freedom fighters, just as you may also speak for those the freedom fighter is attacking. On behalf of the authorities, you might say to the attackers: "I am trying to hear your message, but I need a moment to recover from the pain you have inflicted or I will become vengeful myself."

Then, speaking for the freedom fighter, you might say, "I call you all oppressors to get you to re-examine certain issues right now."

Don't expect the terrorists to be thankful, even if the process of representing both sides is a success. They won't necessarily stop their attacks when the people attacked demonstrate interest in their problems. They want to see action, not just interest. Freedom fighters are irritated by those with social power who wait sluggishly, expecting the attackers to create the social change.

You will have to point out to the terrorists that the mainstream people do not grasp their role in the present process. Then you will have to point out to the mainstream that they should consider taking initiative in repairing what they have inadvertently done.

HELPING THE MAINSTREAM UNDERSTAND

Since terrorists are not always aware that they are causing pain, accusing them of it won't help. In fact, expecting them to understand others' pain will exacerbate the problem. Such understanding can exist only between groups with equal social power. Terrorists may experience others' pain as insensitive, inflated, racist, adultist or sexist. In their view, feeling and understanding others people's pain is a luxury they cannot afford. They want others to realize how they have been made to suffer. Terrorists feel that a marginalized person suffers from social problems the mainstream cannot comprehend.

Sometimes it's helpful to ask mainstream people to think of their personal problems and then imagine adding the extra problems people have due to social rejection and minority status. Remember your own abuse stories. Think about how the mainstream pressures you to behave like a mainstream person. Now consider how people who are not in the mainstream feel.

TO UNDERSTAND FURY, REMEMBER HISTORY

People do not become rigid, abusive or fundamentalist out of the clear blue sky. Individuals and groups that behave abusively to one another have often been badly hurt. This is not an excuse, but it establishes the social context.

When Jews conflict with Jews around Israeli politics today, onlookers must remember the Holocaust and the need to abreact their pain and suffering. Remember that Israelis who have been oppressive to Arabs sometimes acted out of blind rage because of hurts from the past. Remember that before present-day Israel came into existence, Jews had no homeland. Remember, too, when Arab countries are accused by the West of terrorism, that Arabs today suffer from racism the world over.

Give U.S. Blacks who seem anti-semitic the same understanding. Remember that the nation of Islam, which sometimes speaks against Jews, has done much good for the Black community. Remember that the nation of Islam, which is reeling from so much abuse itself, cannot help but compensate by attacking other minority groups. Remember, when Blacks seem unwilling to negotiate with whites, that they are coming from a history of subjection to around-the-clock oppression, violence and racism.

Remember that women who fight with other women over feminist issues have been subjugated for thousands of years. Show more tolerance when women lose their patience with men. Yes, men suffer too, but white men have more overall social power than women. Remember, too, that when ethnic minorities the world over conflict with one another, it's safer than conflicting directly with the mainstream, which resembles hurling the only remaining spear toward the sky. Remember history. Remember that those who have been hurt have always had to enlighten the mainstream — until now. Until someone understands the terrorist, enabling us all to transform together.

NOTE

1. *The Journal of Humanistic Psychology*, Vol. 32, No. 4, Fall 1992, pp. 138-146.

7

The Facilitator's Abuse Issues

FACILITATORS EXPERIENCE mysterious emotions, fear, anger and numbness when working with groups and large organizations. That's because group processes bring up abuse issues from the past. Understanding your own psychology better will make you a more effective facilitator by helping you (1) be sensitive to others, (2) remain centered and not go into shock when you are attacked, and (3) maintain equanimity and provide the group with a sense of safety when the group looks to you for protection in stormy times.

Moreover, being aware of the abuse you have undergone is a general health issue. It is crucial to illness-prevention. Abuse issues affect everyone's health. If you have repressed the pain from past conflicts, it is likely to turn up in body symptoms. Or it creates drug abuse, which further represses pain. Repressed pain from the past often leads to repressing pain in the present. That results in people's overcompensating by getting tough, overworking or despairing.

Abuse work is crucial to crime-prevention. When, for instance, teenagers repress past hurts, they easily become depressed, moody and angry. They think the world is too big or too brutal for them to succeed. They respond to this injustice with violence.

STAYING SENSITIVE TO ALL SIDES

In a recent training for facilitators from large businesses, I saw how a facilitator's abuse issues got in the way of her work with an organization. The woman was an organizational development adviser. She brought me a video tape of work she had done in her company before she was fired. We looked at the tape together. I noticed that, during a conflict session, she had a little secretive smile each time a male secretary argued with the top manager. The manager, a woman, reacted by threatening to fire both the facilitator and the secretary. The secretary seemed to me to have excellent ideas and to present them in a useful manner. Why did the facilitator smile when the boss was attacked?

By way of experiment, I said, "Try smiling freely now and see if you can find out what you were smiling about."

She welcomed the chance to understand herself better. After a while, she said shyly that the boss, even though she was a woman, had reminded her of her father, whom she did not like. She went on to tell me dreadful abuse stories from her childhood. She said she realized that the boss was not her father, yet for some reason she could not separate the two.

I pointed out that the manager was, after all, the boss in an organization that was not particularly democratic; this in itself might be enough to bring up her abuse issues. She said my insight was useful, but insisted that her past was still bothering her in the present. So we decided, since she had already been fired from her job, to focus mainly on innerwork, which would help her be more sensitive to all sides in future conflict resolutions.

THE FIRST STEP: FIGHTING OFF FEAR AND NUMBNESS

Almost everyone who lives or works in a place of conflict is abused by the overall situation. People go numb or become chronically angry, since these are their only defenses against the pain. Belfast and Beirut are not the world's only conflict zones. Almost every home is one. Many of us grew up without a "safe zone," a place to go that was conflict-free. We became bitter, depressed, repressed or numb. We were made into potential terrorists.

As a worldworker, almost by definition, you must be recovering from social and personal oppression. If you weren't, you wouldn't be sufficiently interested in oppression to become a facilitator. Likewise, most psychotherapists have wounds that are healing. Moving through your own pain and suffering is an inevitable preparation for changing the world, and perhaps the best one.

Innerwork begins by learning to be aware of when you need it. Notice when you feel either nothing at all or fear and pain. These are strong indications that you are upset by something inside and/or a terrorist attack from the outside. When you are attacked, you become numb to protect yourself against further pain. The attackers themselves may be numb from having been abused or oppressed; they are incapable of being sensitive to anyone else. The very numbness that once helped you to survive an attack by not feeling it now propagates abuse by blinding you to attack. You unconsciously perpetuate terrorism by not addressing it.

If you notice fear and numbness, stay aware. Allow yourself to feel your feelings. Ask yourself, "How much of this is coming from others, and how much is me?" If you don't ask, your numbness makes you respond to outer situations without thinking. Then you assume that others are your opponents, the bad guys. Since many of us — terrorists, mainstreamers and facilitators alike — cannot endure conflict for long, we try to protect ourselves from it by calling the "bad guys" names. We hold fast to polarized moral positions; things are either good or bad, causes are right or wrong. Such blanket judgments indiscriminately cover everyone we do not like; we don't bother with the individual natures of the people we are hating.

Mainstreamers resort to this form of repression in the face of terrorist anger and threats, while terrorists set themselves irreconcilably against the status quo. Soon everyone's ideas sound like simplistic moralizing. It's the facilitator's job to remain sensitive to everyone, to draw distinctions and to encourage people to fine-tune their comments to reflect their precise feelings.

ABUSE AND POSTTRAUMATIC STRESS

Soldiers in both world wars witnessed so much violence and abuse during battle that they were numb when they got home. Medicine referred to this state as "shell shock." Soldiers were anxious, irritable or depressed after they were discharged into civilian life. Later their condition was called "combat fatigue." Today we speak of "posttraumatic stress disorder."

When you are shocked by gunfire or by someone's aggressive behavior, your eyes open wide. Your jaw drops at first, and later tightens up. You may tremble, develop spasms in your stomach and chest, and hold your breath. You try to turn away and forget it. Later, you try to repress what you experienced. At another stage, you cannot stop remembering, obsessing with thoughts and fantasies, suffering from nightmares about situations you can't resolve.

You do not have to have been in a war to experience posttraumatic stress. Any situation that reminds you of past problems you could not solve may strip you of the amnesia that was protecting you from pain and bring on anxiety and depression. When the women's movement studied the history of abuse, it brought to public awareness how women and their suffering had been dismissed by Freud and others of the psychoanalytic community. Women diagnosed as "hysterical" were later found to be suffering shock from abuse and hurt they suffered in their own homes. Judith Herman's *Trauma and Recovery* traces the history of abuse work and its connection to the women's movement and modern psychological theory.

Women authors have also exposed the mistreatment of children in our society. I recommend especially Florence Rush's *The Best Kept Secret: Sexual Abuse of Children,* and Wendy Maltz's *The Sexual Healing Journey: A Guide for Survivors of Sexual Abuse,* which present research showing that sexual abuse of children is almost epidemic.

THE PSYCHIATRIC VIEW OF ABUSED PEOPLE

Just as mainstream psychiatry treats terrorism as indicative of inner problems rather than social injustice, it has largely discounted the social issues around abuse. Most research on abuse has been patterned after Freud and Jung, who dealt with abuse as fantasy, wish fulfillment, projection of infantile sexuality or dream material whose mythic and archetypal images needed to be interpreted.

Contemporary therapists are perhaps more alert to the devastating effects of abuse, but they often succumb to social pressures. Many therapists treat abuse only as an inner issue, believing the outer scene to be a fantasy that occasions the inner experiences. Until now, therapy has not helped people who suffer from abuse both to do innerwork and to move out into the world of social action to inhibit further abuse.

Some therapies, possibly following religious prescriptions, encourage people to forgive those who have abused them. There is, of course, a moment to forgive, but dealing hastily with abuse issues invites those who experienced them not only to forgive but to forget. Forgetting creates insensitivity to one's own pain and blocks a person from taking the necessary steps to avoid further danger. Forgetting supports abuse in all its forms: rape, beating, harassment, racism, ageism, sexism and homophobia, among others.

A DEFINITION OF ABUSE

I define abuse as the unfair use of physical, psychological or social power against others who are unable to defend themselves, because they do not have equal physical, psychological or social power. Whether a process or relationship is abusive depends upon a group's or individual's sense of their ability to protect themselves. This varies from culture to culture. The important thing is to question whether a situation is abusive. This raises everyone's sense of human rights, civil rights, fairness and democracy. Legal decisions about abuse are often too late and serve only to reduce our sense of personal responsibility for human interactions.

Some types of abuse are especially apparent because they depend on the unfair and overt use of physical strength or social power. Other types are more subtle, though just as devastating — teasing, shaming, belittling and mimicking, for instance. Teachers put down children. On the streets we stare at people who are different from us. We can be abusive by ignoring the pain around us. We covertly abuse others when we witness abusive events and don't use our power to inhibit what is happening.

An essential task is to note the social, cultural and psychological settings in which abuse occurs. What social forces are involved? What
are the governing cultural views on relationships? What are the psychological states of everyone involved?

Because what is defined as abuse depends upon the culture,
misunderstandings occur in multicultural meetings. People from
one culture may not understand why people from another feel hurt
at the "slightest" provocation, and the latter may wonder how the
former can be so insensitive.

For example, people from cultures that support expressive, powerful, strong interactions may not understand why people from a different culture feel shamed when they are "mildly" criticized in public.

Likewise, mainstream people rarely understand that their cultural emphasis on their language is abusive to people who speak
this language with an accent or whose own language has been for-
bidden. For example, too few English-speaking Americans remember that Native Americans, immigrants and Africans brought
forcibly into the United States were made to speak English and punished for speaking in their mother tongues.

When you cannot protect yourself from overt, covert or institutional
abuse, you unwittingly internalize your attackers, adopt their style
and accept their criticism. You belittle and repress yourself and end up
feeling worthless without knowing why. After a while, you no longer
notice the negative thoughts you have about yourself; you simply feel
life is not worth living. You may think sometimes about suicide.

The internalized sense of domination, worthlessness and
depression is aggravated by having to continue living in what feels
like an unfair culture, with a government that is not conscious of
what it does. I am thankful to my brother, Carl Mindell of Albany
Medical School, for having shown the similarities between the
symptoms of posttraumatic stress disorder and the effects of long-
term shaming and belittling.[1]

In my observation, any form of ongoing abuse results in PTSD-
type symptoms. *The American Medical Association Encyclopedia of
Medicine* lists the following symptoms produced by chronic abuse:

1. Anxiety about injury from possible future events such as earth-quakes, riot, rape, torture and military combat.
2. Recurring memories or dreams about dangerous events.
3. Sense of personal isolation.
4. Disturbed sleep and concentration.
5. Tough behavior and deadening of feelings.
6. Ongoing sense of shame and guilt in relationship.
7. Depression.
8. Physical symptoms.[2]

Personal isolation may be associated with fear of other people and a constant dread of impending humiliation. Deadening of feeling means that you do not respond to sad or painful things. It is sometimes supported through the use of alcohol or other drugs. Body symptoms may include chronic pain in the ears and throat, sexual and genital problems, skin-thickening or chronic back pain. Other signs that chronic abuse has occurred include hiding, retreating from public situations and fear of standing up and of speaking out.

Panic dreams and sad memories may arise from anxiety about abuse. Depression, not wanting to get up in the morning and feeling exhausted during the day are often connected to painful past events. Confusion, memory loss, going blank, vague-ness, the sudden loss of clarity, not knowing where you are going and not being able to remember your past may also follow abuse experiences. Lastly, vengefulness — the constant "chip on your shoulder" — often points toward an abuse history.

FACILITATING ABUSE WORK IN TWOS

I suggest that anyone who works with groups consider doing the following exercise, especially if you have several of the above symptoms. This exercise not only reveals personal abuse; it also leads to social action and heightened leadership potential. Please bear in mind that the exercise is not a program. Everyone is an individual, and there are no fixed procedures that can be fol-lowed to work out all problems.

I don't recommend that you think of yourself as a "victim" or "survivor" of abuse. Non-process-oriented therapies encourage pathological identifications. Such diagnoses may be useful, but can unintentionally become abusive, for instance, if you have had a hard time defending yourself against "expert" opinions and categories.

The interview outlined below can be done one-on-one, alone or in groups, especially groups interested in social change. The process may take several hours and is not meant to be concluded in one sitting.

The interviewer should remember that people who have suffered abuse have been in situations where they couldn't protect themselves. They may behave pleasantly and try to please instead of consulting their own inner feelings. Don't push anyone to remember past events. Let the interviewee lead the interview. Don't rush; more time taken now means less later. Remember that very few people willingly go back into painful issues. Repression, while uncomfortable, usually hurts less than remembering. Some of us do not want to think about the past because it seems more important to focus on being present now and succeeding today. We also resist speaking about past difficulties if we think that our listeners have not worked on similar problems or if we feel solutions are impossible. As a facilitator, your skill and compassion arise not only from study, but from having worked on yourself.

In the interview that follows, I have envisioned a case in which the interviewee is a woman.

An Abuse Interview

1. *Ask your partner if she feels safe enough to talk about a past abuse issue.* Take the time to let her feel at home with you. Ask her what she needs in order to feel comfortable. No one is willing to reveal a deep issue unless they feel they will be listened to compassionately. Try to make yourself feel comfortable as well. What do you need in order to feel at ease?

2. Once you are both comfortable, ask your partner: *When was the first time you remember being belittled?* Made to feel ashamed? Made to feel inferior? When was the first time you remember being physically intruded upon by others, against whom you could not defend yourself? Which of these questions elicits the strongest response?

As facilitator, remember that most people who have been abused have trained themselves to ignore their pain. They can override their hesitations even about answering these difficult questions, shrug off abuse issues as insignificant and claim that nothing bothers them: it's all meaningless.

Watch how your partner begins her story. If she stutters, coughs, looks away or has trouble remembering, if she says, "I would like to tell you something from my past," but hesitates before speaking, tell her you, too, may not be ready yet to go on. If you go too quickly or press someone who is not ready to open up, you inadvertently recreate the abuse by applying a force that cannot be defended against.

Tell her to respect her hesitation and check whether the timing is right and whether she trusts you.

3. When you and your partner are ready to focus on an issue, ask the following: *Can you remember or imagine what you were like before you were abused?* How old were you? What did you look like? How did it feel to be alive without abuse? Is this part of you that preceded the injury still alive in you? What does she look like today? How does she appear in your life?

4. *Have your partner choose just one abuse scene to recall.* If she cannot, assure her that it's common for someone not to remember anything because childhood was so painful, or because people acted as if everything was fine when she felt deep suffering. Ask her instead if she can recall any abuse she has seen others suffer from. Don't go further into her own past unless she totally agrees.

5. When you and your partner are ready, *direct her to tell her story in detail.* Who was involved? Did the abuse go on everywhere or in a specific place? What seemed to bring it on? What happened afterward?

Storytelling is a central healing ritual among indigenous peoples, and it should be a healthy part of our lives from childhood. But you may have repressed your story in order to find the courage to grow up. Whatever is missing from your life now may be recaptured in stories from the past.

Abuse stories are especially painful and difficult to tell. They require a good listener. No one can tell a story to a wall.

The attitude of a good listener says that it is acceptable to speak about painful situations openly, and it is all right to ask others to help when we are in pain. Good listeners also convey that they are on the storyteller's side. The storyteller may have felt alone when the abuse happened, but now the facilitator can help break through that sense of isolation.

Your partner may feel that some of the abuse she has undergone, such as racism, is so obvious that it shouldn't be necessary to describe it. She will probably be angry with you if she thinks you are ignorant of it.

She may feel that her story is shameful or evil. She may be afraid that if she tells it, you won't believe her, or, worse, that the abuse will happen all over again. She may feel nothing and lose track of why she's even telling the story.

If you skillfully lead her deeper into the story, she may suddenly find feelings she did not know she had. It's important that, as facilitator, you remember that it doesn't matter whether you already know a lot about that kind of abuse. Maybe you could write a book on it, but your partner still needs to express her experiences. A good facilitator directs gently, again and again: tell the story, tell the whole story. Please tell what you know, everything you know, even the difficult things. It matters to me.

6. After the story has been told, *take time for feelings. Gently bring her attention to moments in the story when she hesitated, became shy or seemed embarrassed.* See if she has more story to tell around those moments.

Sometimes it takes months to tell the whole story, because your partner has lost touch with the pain of it. Encourage her to tell it, and tell it again, until all the feelings are out. Don't stop too early and start analyzing. Your partner needs to go through the emotions in order to make everyday life worthwhile. Emotional release may also relieve any psychosomatic symptoms she may have.

7. *Find the missing truth and myths.* Ask the storyteller to imagine, fantasize, go beyond what she's certain of and tell the vague half-memories associated with the story. She may think that her musings are crazy or unreal. Perhaps she cannot tell the difference between what was fact and what is fantasy, because those around her concealed information. You must take her story to be

reality, for it is her reality. To get to the total reality, she has to reverse her normal thinking. She must dream into what happened in order to tell the missing truths. As she explores her vague recollections, she describes invisible aspects of what was happening, things that did not appear then but were present.

For example, a woman came to see me because she stuttered uncontrollably. When I asked about her possible abuse history, she told me she had been a happy child. Later she hesitantly mentioned that she was not sure whether it was true or not, but she seemed to remember her mother laughing while her father beat her. She talked about her father's abusiveness. After a while, she gained the courage to speak with him directly, which she had to do in fantasy, since he had been dead for some time.

Via fantasy, the truth can be arrived at. Through the fantasy dialogue with her father, this woman discovered that her mother stood by and laughed because she hated her.

Later, when she asked her mother if this was true, the mother confessed that giving birth to a child had been agony and that she had been jealous of the attention her daughter received. The mother had been happy to look the other way when the father abused the child. The mother and daughter fought and wept over the suffering from the past. My client's stuttering abated.

She had internalized the domination and beaten herself, so to speak, for even having feelings about the past. She downed herself the way her father had, and stuttered in fear. She had tried to "look the other way" like her mother; with self-hatred, she hoped to forget her feelings, forget everything. But her stuttering was evidence of her problems. Best of all, she became furious with her self-hatred and began to feel proud of herself instead.

Help your partner create stories and myths around her symptoms that will enable her to find the hidden or missing truths in her life. Tell her: fantasize into the scene; we will discuss reality later.

8. Ask your partner: *who were the witnesses* who neglected your pain and hurt? Who were the third parties who did not intervene?

There are serious social implications in abuse stories because the environment, family system, school system and city are all involved in every abuse situation — even those that occur within the secrecy of the home. If one parent was abusive, where was the other? If both parents were abusive, where were the relatives, the other kids, the neighbors, the school teachers? If the other school children were abusive, where were the teachers and parents? If the school was abusive, where was the family? If the whole city was abusive, where was the government? If the entire government was abusive, where was the rest of the world? If the whole world was abusive, where was God? What kind of societies have our cultures produced?

Asking about witnesses will relieve her of the feeling that she should have done better. It will help her realize others had responsibility for what happened. We all share responsibility for what happens. Passive witnesses are conspirators. Ask, who could have been an active witness when you were being hurt?

Encourage the storyteller, when she is ready, to call those witnesses together and discuss things. Create a family ritual at holidays, funerals, births and marriages. Tell her to ask her relatives: Where were you all when I was being abused? I hope you will intervene in your own and other people's lives, starting now. What were your problems? Why didn't you help? Were you unaware of how I suffered? Wake up and stop abuse from happening!

9. Ask the storyteller: *how was power used against you?* What role did social, spiritual or psychological rank play in the abuse? Were direct and indirect threats made? Can you identify the abusers? Did the abusers act insanely? Was it impossible or even dangerous to defend yourself? Was there a threat of losing someone's love and care if you told the truth? In what ways were you dependent on the abuser(s)? Do you still feel this dependence? Is this one reason why it is hard to tell the story?

Was your youth, your position in the community, or your lack of physical strength used against you? Is the abuse story one of the reasons you are sometimes afraid to talk about yourself? Do you fear other people today? Were you unable to defend yourself against slander and gossip? Was community pressure involved? Was subtle power involved, threats of losing the love of God or the protection of the Church, Synagogue or Mosque or the safety of a spiritual community?

Was there a threat of being kicked out of the community? Was there racism, sexism, homophobia, ageism, anti-semitism or prejudice against a disability? Was the occult involved? It is important for the one who experienced abuse to realize how power was utilized in such a way as to inhibit her from defending herself. She may sometimes feel responsible for what happened if she does not realize how much power others used against her.

10. Ask the storyteller: *what would you do today if you were witness to a similar abuse?*

Follow her process. Assuming that the storyteller has taken the time to think about her story, and assuming that you are interested in going further, you must assess where you are. Ask if it is possible to confront the abusers or witnesses in real life. Can she do it alone or would she like support from friends or from you, a group or community? Would she like to take social action to sensitize others to this problem so it doesn't happen to them or their children?

Perhaps she needs to work further on herself. She may want to go back to the story and tell it again, playing it out by being the different figures in the story. As the story is replayed, she may find a lot of energy from taking the role of the abuser. Frequently, missing powers are projected onto the abuser. She may have promised herself never to be brutal, authoritative or tough like her abusers, yet that tough energy may be exactly what she needs today. Used consciously, it can work miracles.

Or she may suddenly discover that, in fact, she is more like the abuser than she dared to admit. Perhaps she is like the abuser in the way she seeks vengeance.

What does her story explain about her life today? What types of people does she avoid? Which institutions? In what ways is she abusive to herself and others? Does she ever feel like the victim or the abuser in personal relationships? How does her story explain the structure of her interests in the world?

11. *Connect the abuse story to current body symptoms.* Are there special areas of her body that feel injured? How might this be connected with her abuse story? Could the abuse have hurt her physically? What fantasies or worries does she have about those areas?

She may have developed symptoms in areas where her expression was blocked, such as throat, voice, eye and skin problems. Numbness, eating problems, nausea, difficulty swallowing or loss of appetite are often connected to physical and psychological abuse. Sexual problems such as the inability to get aroused or constant sexual stimulation, pain in the groin or chest, and heart pain are some of the many symptoms tied to abuse. Gynecological and prostate problems are often experienced in connection with an abuse issue.

In the experience of these symptoms, there are often reactions, emotions, defenses and guidance that could be of great help in healing the abuse. If she feels or imagines she may have been injured in a certain body area, tell her to pay attention to it, listen to it, feel it, be caring and attentive to it. If necessary, recommend doctors or body workers who are expert in dealing with pain. My books, *Working with the Dreaming Body* and *Working on Yourself Alone* may provide some help.

Find out if she feels that going to a medical professional or body worker may reconstellate the abuse issue. I have worked with hundreds of people around the world on their physical and psychosomatic symptoms. Probably one quarter of the symptoms were connected to abuse stories.

12. *What are the social aspects of her story?* Were the abusers jealous, crazy or just stupid? Who gave them the freedom to hurt her? How old were they? Were they trying to gain revenge for something from their own past? Were they part of her culture or from other cultures? What role, if any, did gender, race or religion play in their abusive behavior? Who is responsible for having supported their behavior? Were brutal models involved? What was happening in the world at that time?

The benefits your partner gets from personal work will always be incomplete without taking social action. Psychological or inner-work must stress social action in order not to propagate abuse. Western therapy has much to learn from the African shaman who advised Pearl Mindell, my sister-in-law, when she was working in Zimbabwe. The shaman told her to reclaim her female power by going back home and getting together all the women, old and young, in her family, and discussing where their female powers had gone.

This African healer knew that personal abuse issues are group issues. Let the women, the men, the whole family, different cultures gather to regain the power of community, consider abuse and determine what to do about it.

Seen in social perspective, individual abuse situations occur because of the way our families and culture allow us to relate to one another. Often, there was no awareness of what was happening, no red light appeared to stop the hurt. When we have a red light that says, "Be careful, that hurts," we will also have green lights that tell us, "Now it's time for all of us to wake up and go forward, noticing hurt, anger and power."

By working on our own abuse issues internally and externally, we help launch a new phase of history in which we will all create culture, this time consciously and together.

NOTES

1. Carl Mindell, "Shaming," lecture at Albany Medical School, New York, 1992.
2. *The American Medical Association Encyclopedia of Medicine,* p. 811.

8

Public Abuse
& Finding Your Voice

PUBLIC ABUSE SHARES some of the characteristics of private abuse, but instead of being hidden and cloaked in silence, public abuse is out in the open where it can be witnessed by millions of people. Public abuse is supported by, even created by, governmental policy.

Forms of public abuse range from blatant to subtle, from premeditated to careless acts. They all violate people who cannot defend themselves. At one end of the spectrum are slavery, torture and public execution. At the other are economic and social infringements of human rights, which are "accepted" and not recognized as abuse.

The national and foreign policies of even democratic nations, which claim to protect their citizens' freedom, can allow infringements of individuals' rights through racism, sexism and other prejudices. People might be theoretically equal in the eyes of the law, but they certainly are not in the eyes of the majority with its mainstream power.

Public policy would cease to be abusive if it helped us see how our unconscious sense of rank recreates inequality every day. As a first step, people would be made aware of the symptoms of public abuse in those who have experienced it: fear of participating in groups, numbness, depression and violence.

Who is to blame? In the United States, according to FBI statistics, someone is violently assaulted or murdered every seventeen seconds. The vast majority of "criminals" are from marginalized or ostracized groups. Violent reaction is their first line of defense.

Public policy should remind everyone that violence originates in abuse. Everyone who witnesses abuse and says nothing is to blame for it. We must awaken the mainstream and empower the poor, young people and other neglected groups. For example, mainstream banks contribute to abusive trends by denying loans to people from minority groups. Supermarkets in minority neighborhoods carry substandard products and charge more than supermarkets in the suburbs. Many city services such as garbage pickup and bus service are worse in minority neighborhoods. Only one percent of public service contracts go to minorities in a town with a 24 percent minority population.

Who is witness to these abuses? All of us. We must create equal educational and job opportunities for disenfranchised people, of course, and we must also inform ourselves about abusive policies that are supported by money interests and police brutality. Understanding the connection between race and economics is not simple. When the Process Work Center of Portland, Oregon, sponsored a city forum, "Race and Economics," big businesses at first resisted sending representatives. Some of them justified their intention of not participating by pointing out that a bank had recently been attacked in the media for being racist. That is, they didn't propose to change their racist policies, only to hide them better.

ABUSE BECOMES COVERT PUBLIC POLICY

Because we are witnesses of public abuse, each and every one of us is guilty of provoking the "criminal" acts of "others." It takes an almost heroic effort for an individual witness to stand up and protest. At a women's convention for equal rights in 1851, a Black woman who had been born into slavery listened as men dominated the discussion. Her name was Sojourner Truth. Finally she rose and spoke these now famous words:

That man over there says that woman needs to be helped into carriages and lifted over ditches. Nobody ever helps me into carriages, or over mud puddles, or gives me any best place. And ain't I a woman?

Look at my arm. I have plowed, and planted, and gathered into barns, and no man could head me!

And ain't I a woman? I would work as much and eat as much as a man, when I could get it, and bear the lash as well. And ain't I a woman?

I have borne thirteen children and seen 'em most all sold off to slavery, and when I cried out with my mother's grief, none but Jesus heard me. And ain't I a woman?

Who should answer her? If you do not, you witness public abuse and help perpetuate it by silence. Sojourner Truth spoke for Black Americans, for women and for all individuals who suffer because they are treated as though they had no rights and no value. The rest of us are numb to our pain and the pain of others. We no longer stand up and complain. If the majority finds itself benefiting from the abuse of others, the abuse becomes chronic and systematic. Racism, anti-semitism, sexism and homophobia are not random; they are covert public policy.

SYMPTOMS OF PUBLIC ABUSE

Parents, teachers, business people, politicians and everyone else who is a leader or facilitator must know the symptoms of public abuse. Public life cannot be democratic if people's pain and dread of abuse prevent them from exercising their freedom of speech, freedom of dissent and freedom to love one another.

Here is a partial list of symptoms I have seen.

Withdrawal, silence and fear. The subjects of public abuse withdraw to prevent further hurt. They don't come to the classroom or the meeting place, and will not vote.

When they do speak, fear is the first message. Fear of speaking up is usually due, not only to the current situation, but to past experiences of being exposed in public and being unable to defend ourselves. Fear of failure may also give rise to a reluctance to speak in public. People are damaged by educational systems that aim at perfection. Many Japanese, for example, feel they must speak perfectly if they are to speak at all. Other people fear speaking because they don't have a command of the mainstream's standard dialect.

Some ethnic groups encourage silence. There are individuals who have a penchant for silence. Others wish to remain neutral. Some people resist being rushed. As a facilitator, you shouldn't leap to the conclusion that every quiet person has been abused. Nevertheless, people who have been personally or publicly hurt usually experience a block when they are asked to voice an opinion.

Since an open forum is an experiment in deep democracy, its success depends upon making everyone feel that their views are important, which in turn requires that everyone participate. It's crucial in meetings to take the time to ask silent people for their opinions and their help. It is also important to help those who ask for help in recovering from their fear.

Speaking out all the time. Some people compensate for past experiences, when it wasn't safe to speak out, by talking incessantly in the present, when it is safe. This, too, may be a signal that the speaker has been badly hurt in the past.

Incongruent consensus. Groups that have been publicly abused may not be able to agree on a focus or consent to a leader's decision. Passivity and apathy may indicate a history of abuse. Democratic countries and organizations do not function well, in part, because people who are afraid or hopeless do not represent their viewpoints. Unless everyone speaks out freely, a consensus is meaningless.

Excessive adaptation. Being "good" may be a symptom of public abuse. Abuse, whether public or private, physical or psychological, forces you to doubt your own realities and feel you are wrong, bad, and worthless. You go along with the flow of things, keep silent because dissent could get you into trouble and take no risks for fear of retaliation. For some disenfranchised groups, under democracies as well as in totalitarian regimes, it is safer to deaden feelings, repress needs and adapt with apparent equanimity.

I recall a woman in Moscow who smiled while being attacked during a group process. At one point, I asked her how she was able to smile. She told us that she had been beaten regularly by her mother-in-law. She learned that she should not fight

Goodness can be a survival technique

back because the mother-in-law must not, under any circumstances, be hurt or criticized.

"Why not?" I asked. The woman smiled and changed the subject. I decided to respect her decision to say no more in front of the group, but I met her after the meeting and discovered that she had been severely beaten by members of her church for not obeying its rules. She had decided at an early age to practice "turning the other cheek" to survive public abuse.

Rigid goodness has deep roots. Facilitators must recognize it as a survival technique.

Fear of ghosts. Public abuse often gives rise to ghosts — powers that are felt but cannot be seen. For example, in Eastern Europe in the early 1990s, even after the KGB had been dismantled, many people feared the "dictator," the "secret police" and spies, who, even though not physically present, were sensed and feared like invisible, brutal ghosts. People constantly checked their rooms and the telephones to see if their private interactions were being monitored.

ghosts

Fear of ghosts is always somehow true. It comes from public abuse in earlier times, but usually it is also connected to polarities not represented in the field right now. The KGB is no longer in operation, but in Eastern Europe people still censor or police themselves. That is why speaking out against dictatorships is so difficult today for many Eastern Europeans who were hurt by the Soviet regime.

But dictatorships are not easily removed. A cab driver in Warsaw told Amy and me that the new democratic government was a worse dictator than the Communists because of its "witch hunt" against old party leaders. He complained that the new government did not provide social security and health insurance. This man overlooked great gains because the dictatorial ghost was still present.

In countries where there has been a secret police or an overt dictator, ghosts are relatively easy to identify. But similar dominating and repressive ghosts are everywhere at any time. Even though they are invisible, you can feel abusive powers because they make the public atmosphere tense and humorless. You notice their existence because there is no laughter, no fun. People are silent, grim and watchful. They do not know where the abusive powers are. They adapt by being quiet, repressing their ideas and/or turning passive and grim.

Infighting and subgroup tension. If your family or group is oppressed by chronic public abuse, it may experience continual conflict, internally and with other groups. Groups internalize the criticism of the oppressor, just as individuals do. They use mainstream criticism against themselves and suffer from bouts of depression and anger as a result.

Some members side with oppressive mainstream views and criticize the rest of the group. Others rebel. This polarity mirrors the external oppression. It is an internalization of the outer conflict and divides the group. For example, Native American communities I have worked with tend to be polarized between those who want more assimilation into the mainstream and those who favor native separation. In the Jewish community, there are those who want to hide their Jewishness, while others are proud of it. In the United States, there are similar conflicts within the Latino, Black, Asian, lesbian and gay, and other communities.

Conflicts go round and round in the oppressed group partly because of the attitude of the mainstream, which looks in through the eyes of the media and sees troubled "minority people." What the media does not tell us, however, is that "minority group" tensions are holographic. That is, they are pictures of tensions that are ubiquitous. Since the mainstream refuses to deal with these tensions, it is more than pleased to project them onto minorities.

Less powerful groups cannot challenge the mainstream for fear of reprisals. They must repress their conflict with the mainstream and focus on their own internal conflicts that mimic it. Or minority groups battle each other, which is safer than taking on the mainstream. The media, once again, aggravates the situation by sensationalizing and exaggerating the conflicts among minority groups. Media reports justify the mainstream view that minority groups are mixed up, irrational, lazy, violent and irresponsible.

Finally, disenfranchised groups are driven to revenge; then the evening news broadcasts images of "extremist" and "criminal" behavior.

We media consumers must wake up to all this. We must realize that disenfranchised groups are working on problems the mainstream neglects within itself. We must understand that these groups behave as they do in reaction to our unconsciousness. The anger they feel toward the mainstream for oppression, they redirect toward themselves. Internal conflict then leaves group members feeling hopeless. They have symptoms of exhaustion, unaccounted-for pains and high blood pressure. In the United States, African Americans are many times more likely to die from heart disease than are whites.

INNERWORK ON PUBLIC ABUSE: BURNING YOUR WOOD

Open forums are an excellent setting for bringing awareness to these problems and to the symptoms of public abuse. Group process within open forums can change organizations and public policy. If you want to work on public abuse alone, within yourself, or as a preparation for such meetings, try "burning your wood."

I learned this expression from an Israeli woman who, after hearing her compatriots continuously lash out at each other and at the Germans at an open meeting in Tel Aviv, said that they were so harsh because they had not "burned their wood." She said that until they did, their ability to resolve the issues was limited.

She meant that there was an overload of dead wood, of potential fuel for anger. People did not realize that this fuel could transform anger and release emotions. The following exercise will help you burn your wood.

1. *Remember a time when you lost your clarity speaking in public or felt your views were not important.*

I met a woman who was an "Untouchable" when Amy and I were working in Bombay. During a group discussion, she remained quiet and looked sad. When we took a break, I asked if she was quiet because that was the respectable thing to do, or if she was afraid of speaking up. She began to tremble. I said she need not answer. She told me that she was afraid to speak because of her heredity. Since childhood, wherever she walked, people had cleaned the floor after her to avoid contact with her defilement. Who could be interested in her or what she had to say? I worked with her, using techniques from this exercise.

2. *What was the first or worst time you were abused in public?* How old were you? Were you shamed or criticized because you were unable to follow public rules; because you were a girl or woman, a boy or man; because of your religion, skin color, ideas, sexual orientation or intelligence; because of health issues, mental or physical abilities or disabilities; by your family, peers, school, town, newspaper or government? Give a name to your experience.

3. *Discuss and/or reenact that public abuse.* Show what happened. If you cannot tell the story in words, try it with puppets or in drawings. What human rights were involved: the right to life, speech, thought, happiness, self-worth, the right to choose a sexual partner from the gender of your choice or the right to be treated as equal with everyone else?

Recall as much of the story as possible. Who was present? How old were you? What group or groups were involved? What was the role of the mainstream? Name the passive witnesses.

What city was this in? Did what happened reflect the times, the milieu in which you lived, the state of the world? How was your experience part of world history?

4. *Using your imagination, what information can you add to the story?* Notice the aspect(s) you emphasize or exaggerate. How is this exaggeration true for you and the community you lived in? How does the exaggeration represent the field of the world you lived in?

5. *Who were the active public abusers?* Why did they do what they did? Is the group they were from still abusing people? What privileges, if any, did your abusers have that you did not have? Where did they learn their behavior? What was driving them to do what they did? Why could they not notice your hurt and stop themselves?

6. *In what ways have you brought the abuse inside yourself and made it private?* Do you hide parts of yourself from the world because you are afraid? Which parts? What physical symptoms do you have now that might have their origins in this painful memory? What do you imagine the public abuse has done to your body?

Do you experience anger, or sadness, or nothing at all about this memory? Give yourself time to notice what you are feeling.

7. *When were you last attacked or shamed in public?* What are the similarities and differences between the earlier episode and this last one? Do you see patterns in your vulnerabilities and reactions?

8. *Now try burning your wood.* Bring back your strongest memory of abuse. Ask someone to play different parts in the story if you need help. Find a good listener and ask that person to keep enough distance to help you in case you go blank and forget your feelings. Tell your story. Tell it again.

The crucial part of this work is to give permission for your pain, sadness, rage, fury and vengefulness to exist. Notice them, feel them and let them be. Do not judge them or try to set them aside.

If you can, without hurting yourself or anyone else, go so deeply into your emotions that an "enantiodromia" occurs, that is, your feelings transform into their opposites. As you move through this process, watch for hesitations, blocking, signals of nervousness, unfinished sentences, numbing, confusion and blanking out. Encourage your helper to ask you if you feel safe, if you have gone far enough or if you want to go further.

9. *Mourn the unfairness of what happened.* Mourn the injustice, the lack of love, the absence of respect, appreciation and caring. Be compassionate with yourself, your anger and your grief. Can you allow rage and vengefulness to arise? Watch for numbness and blanking out. Notice how you forget and suddenly remember. This is due to the state of shock you went into so that you would be able to go on with your life. Have courage. Care about the details of your feelings as you move around and through them. Be sure to name them as they arise and honor them.

If you get stuck, watch for feelings that seem overwhelming, too unrealistic or too embarrassing. Go into them. Do it for yourself; do it for the rest of us.

10. *How have you internalized public abuse that you have experienced?* Do you shame or keep yourself down today by being overly self-critical? In what ways do you behave toward yourself as your abuser(s) did? Do you hurt yourself with disparaging, minimizing and deprecating comments? What do you know about yourself that you would never tell? Can you defend yourself against your own self-criticism?

Tell your story again. Can you feel the abuser's hurtful behavior internalized as tendencies you have to turn against yourself? Do you push yourself too much? Set standards that are too high? Restrain yourself from saying what you want to say in public or repress your feelings?

11. *What ideals did your abusers support?* Was the abuser part of the mainstream or a freedom fighter? What was behind the beating they gave you? Was it the satisfaction of their own lust? Getting back for what happened to them? An attempt to enforce a moral code? How do you feel about their ideals? Do these ideals operate in your life now? For example, if you were shamed for being lazy or not being smart enough, do you now criticize other people for being lazy or push yourself to be "smarter?"

12. *Imagine yourself as the abuser.* If you are uncomfortable feeling the power of the abuser, ask yourself if you are like the abuser at times. Or do you pressure yourself to be the exact opposite of the person or group who abused you? Are any of your powers linked to theirs? Perhaps you are already using the power of the abuser in a wise manner, perhaps not. For example, consider a classic case. Many of us said we would never do to children what our parents did to us. Then, lo and behold, one day we catch ourselves doing just that.

The woman who was an Untouchable told me that at home she could be quite violent, even with the women in her family. She realized that she sometimes acted as mean as the people who hurt her.

13. *Transform the abuser's power.* Is there anything good about the power of the abuser? Can you imagine using that power in a productive way? When I asked the woman from India how she could use the power of that meanness in another way, she said she would now love to be vocal about women's and caste issues. After all, if she was so free to be strong at home, at least she could be courageous enough to speak up in public. The possibility seemed to thrill her.

When the meeting reconvened, she became one of the main speakers, encouraging others to bring up taboo topics. She later wrote me that she had succeeded in raising her family's consciousness about women's and caste issues.

What might you accomplish with your strengths? Imagine yourself achieving those goals.

14. *Find your spirit and your voice.* People who have been hurt by private and public abuse often have dreams that contain powerful wisdom or guidance. Can you recall such dreams? Have you had visions of helpful spirits, gods or goddesses?

One name shamans have for such inner figures is "familiars," spirits who bring human beings wisdom they cannot find anywhere else. In my book *The Shaman's Body*, I call these helping spirits "allies" in accordance with shamanic traditions the world over, including the one described by Carlos Castaneda. You may think of allies as God, Buddha, the Self, your own wisdom or guardian angels. Whatever you call these guides, whether you feel they are within yourself or in the environment, their assistance puts great powers at your disposal. Such powers are gifts of spiritual rank which allowed you to survive abuse. They will help you to find your voice.

Try to remember or feel these powers now. Imagine their presence. Speak to them, or listen. Ask them about yourself and about the world. Ask them to give you a hint about what your particular world task might be. Consider the possibility that this task is one of the purposes of your life.

Indigenous people throughout the world have always had spirit guides who helped when human beings could not. They facilitate transitions in times of crisis. In dreams, they awaken your shamanic powers and show you the way to heal public abuse. Your visions are images of healing spirits who are benevolent ghosts. These are the powers behind your voice in the world.

9

How Good Societies Make War

GOOD SOCIETIES MAKE WAR. Democratic societies that believe they have a policy of non-aggression are guilty of public abuse.

It happens in:

Family gatherings, where certain people are put down for not meeting a subgroup norm.

Schools that belittle children for breaking the rules and that teach only mainstream values and history, ignoring non-mainstream values and styles of communication.

Businesses that succeed economically at the expense of the environment, minority groups, and the needs of individuals.

Civil Service organizations, such as the police, that harass minority groups.

Newspapers that don't report information of concern to marginalized groups.

Media that either portray minority groups in negative stereotypes such as the criminal or the unreliable employee, or ignore minorities and reflect only the lives of the dominant population.

Banks that favor the mainstream businesses of the middle and upper classes.

Religious groups that threaten punishment for "sinners" or otherwise make non-members feel they have no chance of liberation.

Medical systems that ignore the feelings of patients.

Psychology that claims states-of-mind to be independent of social issues and views people who are different from the mainstream as sick.

Worldworkers-in-the-making need to know that this is only the beginning of a laundry list because public abuse is pervasive. No area of life is safe from it.

QUIET AGGRESSION

To be sure, what is considered abuse or personal harm is a matter of culture. Whether a culture believes human rights are given by God or thinks they are conferred by law or by people, there's one thing we know: human rights are necessary because people are vulnerable.

The list of ways people can be publicly abused is an indication of the breadth of our vulnerability. We need eldership and protection on every front. We need food, clothing, housing, and medical care. We need respect and protection from one another. We are social beings and need the company of others. We are teleological beings and need meaning.

Governmental laws do not provide these protections effectively because they cannot make lack of awareness in personal interactions a crime. Religions step in where governments fail. In Buddhism, for example, rights are interconnected with duties: survival depends on everyone's preserving life. Buddhists accord rights to animals, plants and inert objects, since souls may have been reincarnated in those forms.

In Judaism, too, rights and duties are interdependent. In the end, all duties are to God. But many involve the care of human beings, who are often collectively symbolized in the Jewish scriptures as "the widow and orphan." In Christianity, to love God is to love the person next door. One of the five pillars in the practice of Islam is helping the needy. Rights in the Baha'i religion come from endowments of qualities and powers given by God. Indigenous people believe everything is a spirit and vulnerable.

In practice, though, religions often fail as the protectors of human rights because too few of us know what to do with the abusers besides saying "no" or punishing them. Moreover, many spiritual views of human rights are anthropocentric. We need a cosmotheandric vision — that is, one that includes gods, people, animals and the whole environment.

In my concept of deep democracy, rights aren't just a matter of being allowed to vote and having representation in Congress. Deep democracy happens in face-to-face interactions as well. It requires awareness, which is prior to freedom. Without awareness of how power is used and how unconscious rank oppresses people, the legal concept of equality has little meaning.

Equality, not only in economic matters but in personal ones, begins with education about power and its abuse. After all, legal rights — even if they were totally enforced — could never fully protect us against invisible powers that are so hurtful. For example, *The Oregonian*, Oregon's largest newspaper, recently published a story about a bank's "invisible" policy of refusing small loans to potential homeowners in certain areas. This policy was directed toward Blacks and other groups of little power, who were thereby forced to continue renting.

Denying home-ownership is an invisible act of aggression that enforces segregation and supports rank for the wealthy. This is a hidden form of public abuse, an example of how peaceful societies carry on quiet wars against those who cannot defend themselves.

DEMOCRACY IN ACTION: MUDSLINGING AND COURTROOM PAIN

In democratic countries, politicians are allowed to engage in public abuse as a campaign or lobbying strategy. It's called "mudslinging" — making demeaning personal remarks about the opponent. This tactic ensures that we select our country's chief executive on the basis of who has the speech writer with the greatest ability to tear down other people's characters.

Public abuse goes hand in hand with an adversarial legal system whose goal is to determine who's right and who's wrong instead of how to improve relationships. An adversarial system supports power, supports right and might rather than understanding and connection to others. An adversarial system works toward increasing conformity and productivity, not compassion.

Think about criminal court proceedings. Instead of disseminating understanding of a defendant's position in the entire social context, our courts only determine guilt or innocence. Court proceedings are carried out with no concern for their overall effect on the "criminal" or the "victim."

The Navajos have a non-adversarial, community-oriented legal system. The conflicting parties meet with one another and are free to say anything they want without an authority determining who is right and who is wrong.[1] Relatives are included in the process, and the relatives of the one who causes injury are considered among those responsible for the crime. They, too, must compensate the injured party. The relatives of the injured party are entitled to compensation along with the victim. Well-being for all is placed before attribution of blame and punishment. This system is based on community, relationship and interaction instead of right and wrong, good and bad.

We support badgering of witnesses in our courts and mudslinging in the political arena for the same reason we watch violent films. Our culture is hungry for heroes and heroines who risk their lives for the sake of vengeance. We look for bullies who model self-defense and destroy their opponents. Why? Because we have abuse issues that have not been worked out; because we have been hurt and could not defend ourselves.

What can the worldworker do? Notice and support leaders who show us how to deal with conflict and pain through awareness. We must break the cycle of vengeance and mudslinging by insisting that all sides not only be heard, but be present when the other side speaks. We must notice double signals and strong feelings, anything that moves us beyond the superficiality of innocent or guilty, right or wrong.

WHAT LIES BEHIND SILENCE

In any diverse group, there are likely to be a few individuals who say nothing. As a facilitator, take the time to investigate silence.

Ask the person, "Are you silent because you enjoy silence? Do you believe in your feelings? What are your feelings and responses to others? Would you like to contribute, but feel afraid?"

When the atmosphere is tense and uncomfortable, speak in private to people who have been silent. Back in the group, without criticizing, suggest possible reasons for the tension. Ask everyone to be silent. Ask whether people feel good about their silence. Ask if the group feels safe or unsafe. When things feel unsafe, some people behave with subservience. Everyone makes a show of surface politeness.

I remember a good example of this in the ex-Soviet Union. I was at a large conference devoted to solving ethnic tensions. During an intermission, I attended the showing of an amateur film by Ingustians about how they were attacked by their neighbors, the Ossetians. We saw a bloody, horrible street massacre.

At the end, one speaker said furiously that the Ossetians were supported and provoked by the Russians. The room of about a hundred people was hushed. After many painful minutes of silence, I stood up in the middle of the crowd and asked the quiet woman next to me what she was feeling. "Horror," she whispered into a microphone. "Horror. I hate killing."

When I asked if anyone else felt something, no one spoke. It seemed as if everyone was afraid. So I asked anyone who had the same feelings as the woman who hated killing to move closer to her. To my surprise, more than half the audience slowly moved towards the woman, who was in the center of the room. Then I suggested that anyone else who was on the side of the Ingustians move to my right, and those on the side of the Ossetians and Russians move to my left.

Then everyone was surprised. In the middle of the room was a mass of silent people, a clear majority. They were so numerous and so powerful that their very presence could not be ignored by the warring parties on either side. The power of silence was so great and the number of people interested in war so few that the conflict dissolved.

A history of public abuse had made the majority of people afraid of speaking out. They could not raise their voices to protest. Addressing the silence showed that in a terrible conflict, the warring parties are not the center of the battle, but a great number of us who want peace. If we were more present, a lot of conflicts would be resolved more easily.

A good facilitator senses the existence of social abuse, knows history and sees its effects in the present. Moment-to-moment awareness helps groups that may not be used to democratic styles of open debate to process their experiences. If you are in a group where totalitarianism, illness, drugs, violence or fundamentalism are big issues, you might experiment by speaking for those who are silent, for those who are afraid or have been put down.

For example, to those who are silent, you might say, "Notice what you are feeling, it could be useful to us all, so whisper your viewpoint to your neighbor." If no one speaks, you might say for them, "We cannot speak, it is too dangerous for us now."

Proceed with caution. In some circumstances, speaking out might cost individuals their jobs or occasion further public shaming, physical injury or death. People are silent for a reason. Behind silence is fear of the abuse of power. Always consider the possible consequences. Provide enough protection. If necessary, ask people to answer questions in private, on paper or by some other anonymous means.

Don't underestimate the power of the status quo. The ghosts of rank resist answering questions about human rights abuses, even when the organizations or individuals are committed to human rights. Be sure to ask the group — including those who have been silent — for permission to focus on a particular topic, especially if it concerns human rights. Otherwise, some people will feel that you are using your facilitator's rank to force the group to face things it is not ready for.

While making power, rank and hierarchy clear, watch your own tendency to silence people by using your rank as facilitator to oppress those who do not agree with you. If you take the side of the oppressed, you lose the interest and trust of those who have power. In the end, you may not help anyone.

CLARITY OVER RESOLUTION

Most of us hope for resolutions from group discussions of abuse issues. In fact, we all want resolution of our own issues. Yet it's not because we are incapable of achieving resolution that it so rarely happens. Causes may include ambiguous feelings, hidden secrets, personal agendas or a desire for revenge. Those with rank are rarely ready to be enlightened about their powers.

That's why searching for clarity is more sustainable than forcing resolutions before everyone is ready. Resolutions are important, but only within the context of increased clarity. Part of clarity is understanding that almost every conflict is a mixture of social, physical, psychological and spiritual issues.

A participant at one of our conferences was in ill health and used a wheelchair. She asked me to facilitate an argument she was having with her hotel. She had complained about her noisy room so often that the hotel management was asking her to leave. She threatened them with a lawsuit. The hotel manager became furious and complained to me bitterly. The woman turned her head away and refused to negotiate. I told the manager on her behalf that she was using her power to threaten him because, for her, this was not a fair fight. He was the boss of the building she was living in. He was a man; she was a woman. He could walk; she could not. He was on his turf; she was not on hers.

She started listening to what I was saying. I went on stating her case for her: her issue was justice, not finance. Something touched him; he nodded his head slowly. I said that I knew he wanted the best for his business and did not mean to hurt anyone's feelings. I said I knew money was important to him, but that deep underneath, money was not the issue. He too was listening intently. He said that I was right, money was not the only issue for him. He said he understood her, but was afraid of her anger and power.

She smiled. I said, "Let's drop the discussion for now. There may be important feelings that want to happen when each of us is alone." I proposed that we meet later. The manager said that was not necessary and asked the woman to stay. He promised her another room.

This painful confrontation was ended, not by pushing for resolution, but by raising the manager's awareness of the discrepancies in their ranks.

THE GHOST IN THE PAYCHECK

An effective facilitator knows the social issues, including economics. Market-oriented economies, for the most part, abuse the poor and favor those with greater income and wealth. They are *economics?*

responsible for producing inequalities in income, living conditions and employment opportunities. Wealthy individuals contribute to unemployment by discouraging unionization, fixing
minimum wages and exporting manufacturing to poor countries
where labor is exploited. At home, this produces marginalization,
aggression, hopelessness and violence.

As a facilitator, speak about economic inequality and bring
out the ghosts that are present. Few people want to be identified
with the "evil" capitalist. You may have to play the figure at the
top of the economic ladder yourself. The capitalist ghost does not
care about the distribution of basic goods, the equality of services
or work and educational opportunities. He is out for himself.

Although the last part of the twentieth century has witnessed
the overthrow of many harsh regimes, the privatization of industry abuses workers by giving businesses the privileged dictatorial
power that once belonged to governments. Capitalist democracies have suffered from private enterprise all along. They afford
relatively great personal freedom, but they abuse people who are
marginalized due to poor education, class, race, gender, sexual
orientation or age.

I have seen organizations change and work efficiently after
meetings in which employees brought up the ghost roles of the
"bosses," who wanted everything for themselves, and the "victims," who wanted equality and justice.

MEDIA ABUSE: MAKING MONEY FROM CONFLICT

Our news is filled with the personal lives of politicians, movie
stars and well-known athletes, who represent less than one percent of the general population.

In capitalist democracies, the media are businesses. Their
products target consumers who have the purchasing power to
buy books, newspapers and magazines as well as items touted in
their advertisements. Such consumers buy stories in which vengeance, slander, mudslinging and violence play central roles.
Thus our purchasing power supports the media's public abuse.

"Alternative" media have contributed to a heightened awareness of the environment, the conflicts in our world, develop-
ments in psychology and trends in spirituality. These media
include New Dimensions Radio in San Francisco and Radio for

Peace International in Costa Rica. I note many valuable "alternative" magazines in the bibliography.

Oppressed groups and conscious individuals who have suffered from media distortions have fought back by becoming media people themselves. Sara Halprin and Tom Waugh coined the term "committed documentary" for the cinematic work of these social activists.[2] Women and People of Color who are film-makers, as well as film-makers from countries such as El Salvador, Cuba, Nicaragua, Russia, the Czech Republic and China have made important contributions to our understanding of oppression.

Most media report on "conflicts" showing how "the good guys" beat "the bad guys" or conversely how "the bad guys" win. Adversarialism is a money-maker. It sees the world as a gigantic football game between two sides who have no relationship to one another.

The media love to expose the weaknesses of public figures. But the abusive methods of adversarialism don't correct anything. Media people should do more than bring embezzling politicians, for instance, to public attention. They should show how abuse goes in both directions between the public and its "servants." Both attack one another, and, without facilitators or a fair debate in which the parties are protected, everyone suffers.

As a facilitator, don't lend weight to adversarial democracy by assuring a win for one, or even both, sides. Focus on the relationship between the opponents.

COMBATING CULTURAL BIASES IN THE HELPING PROFESSIONS

Education, medicine and psychotherapy make many judgments on the basis of hidden assumptions. For example, these disciplines lean heavily on modern physics, which assumes that science began with the Greeks and ignores the shamanistic insights into matter and nature that are treasured by all indigenous people.

The Eurocentric judgments of modern science have enormous repercussions for the world. Authority figures such as teachers, doctors and psychologists use their power without checking on its effects. They are often inadvertently abusive to students and patients. For example, disparaging children for their lack of interest or inability to learn specific educational forms, such as mathematics or science, hurts everyone.

The Diagnostic and Statistical Manual of the American Psychiatric Association (DSM IV), under diagnosis number 313, states that the diagnosis "Oppositional Defiant Disorder" applies to children who frequently do any four of the following things for six months: lose their temper, get furious with adults, refuse to comply with adult rules, annoy others, blame others for their misbehavior, or act angry or spiteful. This diagnosis assumes that the adults in the situation are innocent and that children should be compliant rather than stand up for their interests. How can a ten-year-old child argue with such a diagnosis?

Calling someone a "bad" patient because of his or her refusal to go along with the doctor's recommendations is a judgment that rests on the belief that patient cooperation should be the norm. Since this assumption is not articulated, the patient cannot raise a defense.

Doctors and psychiatrists speak from the safety of mainstream privilege when they label disenfranchised people's rage as inappropriate behavior stemming from a sense of inadequacy or other psychological problems. Diagnoses of symptoms as paranoid, delusional or psychosomatic turn people against their own feelings. A vicious cycle is set up; marginalized groups become self-destructive and enact the craziness with which they are stigmatized. After the "authorities" have pronounced their diagnoses, it takes a lot of power for minority individuals to dare and believe that their rage is provoked by mainstream avoidance of social problems and not by psychological peculiarities of non-mainstream groups.

Since psychology and psychiatry help many people, it is difficult to imagine that they also hurt people. Yet, in *Racism and Psychiatry*, Alexander Thomas and Samuel Sillen detailed the painful history of racism in modern psychiatry. For example, the psychoanalytic approach to Black rage claims that it arises from an Oedipal complex. This assumes, first of all, that People of Color relate to the same Greek or European mythology as whites. Secondly, it assumes that Black rage originates in childhood problems rather than in a racist culture.

Jung, following the unquestioned assumptions of European thinking at the beginning of the twentieth century, wrote: "Living together with barbaric races exerts a suggestive effect on the laboriously tamed instinct of the white race and tends to pull it down." Jung felt that Blacks had "infected" whites. "What is more contagious than to live side by side with a rather primitive people?" he wondered.[3]

It is difficult for me to point out unconscious rank in C.G. Jung, whom I love. I agonized for weeks about criticizing him, my favorite teacher, for being blatantly racist, anti-semitic and sexist. But if you and I do not raise such issues, we too become abusive.

Future generations will criticize me, too, for being unconscious of abuse I am not able to see today. They must. Fortunately, sometimes being unconscious of privilege does not mean that everything we do is bad. If Jung were here today, I am certain he would feel sad, and want to learn and change. I know how he loved people. I also know how sad I am when someone makes me aware of things I do that hurt others. I have to remind myself that being right or wrong is not the most important thing. The feelings between us are what count.

As I have pointed out, psychology has been Eurocentric until now. It has supported a publicly abusive culture in the academic world with its assumptions — never overtly discussed — that white behavior is the norm and whites are better than People of Color. Eurocentric thinking says, for example, "Make it alone. Be strong and independent. Tame your emotions," ignoring the reliance on family and community in other cultures and the place of honor they accord their feelings. We need Afrocentric, Australiocentric, Japanese-centered, Native American-centered as well as Eurocentric education if we are to avoid public abuse.

Today mainstream psychological practitioners support the values of the dominant culture by pathologizing rebellion, anger, fury, "infantilism" and "venting" (which is deemed "inappropriate" public behavior). "Consciousness" has become synonymous with reduced affect. Unconscious behavior is popularly referred to as "the shadow," — a concept that implicitly denigrates dark skin.

It's not the words that are the problem, it is the unconscious feelings and assumptions behind the terms. There is no sign of doubt, only certainty, in such generalizations. For example, terms like "emptiness" and "self-knowledge" are not sufficiently inclusive of groups that do not have European backgrounds. Eurocentric concepts such as "acting out" imply that emotional expression (the very core of many cultures) is pathological. Such concepts are merely cultural biases, not truths. Yet Eurocentric generalizations about people and culture are currently accepted worldwide. We need a new multicultural psychology which is not cross-cultural but instead culture-specific.

The popular stress today on "individuation" and the uniqueness of the individual pays no attention to the value of community. In the hands of Westerners, Eastern concepts end up sounding like the Eurocentric emphasis on the supremacy of the individual. Personal "wholeness" is defined without reference to the ability to deal with social issues. The "transpersonal self," that is, the mature self that has transcended the strictures of mere ego, looks for completion in becoming "the face you had before you were born." This favors aspects of us that are outside of time and space; it may negate the importance of our eldership in the midst of multicultural tension.

Maslow's idea of "self-actualization" is too limited today. In his book, *Toward A Psychology of Being*, he described the "developed," self-actualized individual:

> Such a person, by virtue of what he has become, assumes a new relation to his society and indeed, to society in general. He not only transcends himself in various ways; he also transcends his culture. He resists enculturalization. He becomes more detached from his culture and from his society. He becomes a little more a member of his species and a little less a member of his local group.[4]

Mainstream readers may think this sounds perfect. And it may be for them. Others see the use of "he" to mean everyone and will debate or excuse it. But people from disenfranchised groups cannot completely agree with the idea of "detaching from your culture" and being "more a member of your species and a little less a member of your social group." After all, this is what has always been legally forced on or recommended to women, Native Americans, People of Color, gays and lesbians. If they leave their groups any more than they already have, whole cultures, tribes and nations will die.

If Maslow lived now, I am certain he would want self-actualization to mean freedom to choose which culture you want to belong to, or the freedom to stay in or leave your culture, as the

Amy saw him shifting from foot to foot and asked him to speak. "I understand your point," he said, red in the face. "But I still insist I am not racist."

Amy said that his red face could mean he was hurt or angry. "I'm angry," he said. "I am a good man. You don't know me!"

"I'm sorry," I replied. "I wish I had time to get to know you. I believe you are basically a good man. And racism is a dirty word. But if anyone in your family looks down on People of Color and you do not confront your family about this issue, I still think you are racist. You propagate a social system that gives you privileges at the expense of People of Color."

He turned his back on me, shaking his head. I said, "You can, if you want, leave this meeting. You can walk out on this conflict in this room, and even then, you use white privilege. People of Color can never walk out on this problem."

He stood his ground. "I do not agree with you. I love People of Color. That is why I want to spend more time with African Americans and Latinos in the poor sections of the city where they live. I want to get to know them better and help the poor."

"Thanks. Your intentions are good, but not all Blacks and Latinos are poor, and not all the poor are People of Color," I said. "Spending time with People of Color might help you feel better, but it probably will not do much in the long run to combat racism. You are needed just as much or more in your own white neighborhood. Awaken your neighbors and friends to their rank and privilege. In the long run, that will have a greater effect on changing the color of poverty."

He pointed out that some African Americans at the meeting disagreed with me. He quoted them as saying that their problems arose from class and economics. I said, if they disagreed with me, I would like to listen to their viewpoint and learn from them. "But, why," I asked, "do you side only with those Blacks who wish to focus on issues of class instead of race, generously letting whites off the hook? That's how we whites divide their community, by siding only with those who forgive us. Blacks who stress the problem of class are incredible people, and I have a lot more to learn from them. But do you think that if everyone was of the same class, racism would no longer exist? I say it would."

For the first time, he seemed to acquiesce. While he was thinking, I said, "You can visit the world of Blacks, Latinos, Chinese, Indians and Japanese, but this isn't a reciprocal power.

What about African Americans who want to visit a white country club? They might even be arrested for trespassing, no matter how wealthy they are. This has to do with color, not class."

He agreed, but he insisted that, though I had made an excellent point, I had not listened to him. I was so tied up with my viewpoint, I seemed to think he mattered less than a Person of Color. He asked if that's what I really thought. I apologized, and I thanked him.

GOING BACK INTO MY HISTORY OF ABUSE

We resolved our conflict. We were both touched. He was quiet, and I was sad. He had been remarkably humble in saying that he had learned from me. I had learned from him, too. I had asked him to have a heartfulness and awareness I had not been able to extend to him.

I realized I had a lot of "wood to burn" and, after the meeting, went back into the public abuse issues that have troubled me since childhood. I realized that I was fighting for the Blacks, not only because prejudice against anyone is against everyone, but because of my personal story. Years ago, Black kids taught me how to fight and save myself from being hurt on the streets. I was paying them back for that lifesaving gift.

I was born in a small town in upper New York State just as World War II was breaking out. By the time I went to first grade, it seemed as if the whole world around me was anti-semitic. I realized for the first time that I had been born into a Jewish family when other kids called me ugly anti-semitic names and ganged up on me. Black kids taught me how to protect myself in street fights and to come out winning.

Besides learning more about myself, I realized something new about why racism remains such a painful and unaddressed social issue. Whites will grudgingly work to correct sexism because it can be found at home. White men cannot avoid white women. Given a lot of coaxing, mainstream folks will even tackle homophobia, because members of their own families might be lesbian or gay. But when it comes to racism — to the color of the skin — things change. A white couple may give birth to a girl who turns out to be lesbian, but she probably won't turn out to be Black.

Race is bound to remain a most troublesome and very unpopular issue. In the Western and Northern parts of the world, People of Color will continue to take the brunt of mainstream unconsciousness.

The Western white community keeps the politics of race locked into a binary prison of white/color. Whites see the world as made up of "people" and "People of Color." The mainstream blocks itself from working on its unconsciousness by relegating to the periphery issues it supposes are concerns only for People of Color. The mainstream thereby ignores a vital part of its own spirit and deadens the white culture. There are in the United States a few notable exceptions to this numbing trend, for instance, publications such as *The Nation* and *Z Magazine*.

ONLY THE MAINSTREAM IS RACIST

Prejudice devastates minorities and also marginalizes the soul — the emotional and spiritual part — of those who are prejudiced.

Racism is the intentional or unintentional and unconscious use of the mainstream race's political power against another race with less social power.

Racism is a negative value judgment by those races in the mainstream about people of other races. This value judgment legitimizes exploiting and downing others.

According to my definition, only the mainstream can be racist. Mainstream people sometimes refer to social activists who fight for the rights of minorities as "reverse racists." This misses a crucial point. People can be the reverse only when they have equal social power, and nothing short of a miracle or a revolution can accomplish that.

The point of this definition is to differentiate power and to alleviate public abuse. Racism refers to the use of mainstream rank against people who don't have enough social power to defend themselves. Racism is always social abuse.

Facilitators — especially those from the mainstream — must realize that racism is economic, institutional, national, personal, interpersonal and psychological. People of Color are uncomfortable around white people who are oblivious to their economic, racial or psychological rank. Unconscious rank confuses and inhibits communication between the mainstream and people of lesser rank. For example, if you are a white, middle class heterosexual, you may go around assuming that everyone is heterosexual. Homosexuals will not feel free to be themselves in your proximity.

Or, if you are a person of high economic status, you may blithely assume that everyone can afford to eat in upscale restaurants. While you are cool and confident, other people may feel inferior, embarrassed, fearful, or servile around you, or they may adopt a tough facade by way of compensation. I am not suggesting that they don't need to work on themselves; I just want to show you the role you play in their behavior.

Rank- and color-blindness push those with less rank away. Unconsciousness creates segregation, the kind that can't be overcome by laws. Blindness to difference makes others doubt themselves and then come to believe that their lack of confidence or freedom is their own problem.

THE CURTAIN COMES DOWN ON POLARIZATION

As the percentage of People of Color in the world increases, mainstreams everywhere learn that the world cannot be divided into a monolithic "Us" and a monolithic "Them." Latinos and Asians are becoming more numerous in the United States than African Americans. Whites will be in the minority by the mid-twenty-first century. Interracial children weaken the boundaries of the binary system. Nevertheless, history, psychology and politics combine to keep racism alive and thriving. This point is developed thoroughly in the classic text, *Race and Manifest Destiny* by Reginald Horsman.

Our binary thinking polarizes the timespirits in the field and ignores people of mixed ethnicity. We are all polarized to fit those social roles. You become politically identified with the roles or timespirits of your regions; you are pressed to identify yourself solely with one group or another — indigenous, white, Black, Asian or European — even if you don't want to.

Forced to identify with one part of yourself, as when a Black and Vietnamese child is made to identify with either Vietnamese or Black, causes a lot of agony and confusion. A whole country can work with polarizations as if clearly defined categories were involved. Meanwhile, millions of people are left out. Polarization is caused by prejudice, not fact. No one is, for example, simply Black or white. Each of us has a very specific nature and ethnicity.

Though many of us are proud of our ethnicity, others want to be acknowledged as individuals independent of an ethnic heritage. Whether we like it or not, however, we are stereotyped by projections onto our race, gender, religion and sexual orientation.

As a facilitator, you must remember that not everyone fits into one of two neat groups. Battles over race have the purpose of awakening the mainstream to its role in creating ethnic tension. On one level of these battles we encounter ethnic pride; on another, consciousness of difference, all kinds of differences that exist within the ethnic group itself. That is why, when the theme of race is introduced, every other kind of tension may come along in its wake.

NOT BEING RACIST: AN ALL-DAY JOB

What you learned in your history books was misleading. In a democracy, people are not and may never be equal.

For instance, Latinos and Blacks are more likely to be harassed by the police, scrutinized by shopkeepers, denied bank loans and given poor service than are whites. In the United States, if you are Black or Latino and are sitting in an old car in front of a store, chances are a police officer will come along and ask to see your identification. If you are white, sitting in the same car in the same spot, probably no one will notice.

The only way a mainstream person can avoid being racist is to be awake all the time. Or, as Black nationalist leader Kuame Ture said in a radio interview with David Barsamian in 1990, "The only way you can say you are not racist is if you are struggling against racism in every aspect of life!"

When I read Kuame's words in a public lecture once, a white person objected, "Are you crazy? What would my life be like if I struggled against racism in every aspect of it? It sounds exhausting!"

I said, "You learned how to walk, and you use your awareness of walking all day long. If you learn about rank, in time that awareness will become automatic as well."

FAKE COMMUNICATION ABOUT REAL PROBLEMS

Mainstream people expect their own communication style to be universal. Mainstream speakers, represented by people who have advanced educations, use big words, speak reasonably, with confidence and without an accent.

At a town meeting on race and economics that Amy and I facilitated in Portland, Oregon, I asked a white spokesperson from a large bank if there was any racism in the bank. He responded quite sincerely that there wasn't. After all, he said, everyone at his bank had diversity training. They had seen films about how to speak to People of Color.

This demonstrates how the mainstream deals with racism. First of all, you come up with some polysyllabic term that creates emotional distance between you and the people you are supposed to help. You decide you aren't going to talk about racism or prejudice but "cultural diversity." That makes everything antiseptic. After exchanging politically correct clichés, you create a seminar, call it "diversity training," and claim the problem is fixed: there is no more prejudice. In this way, people with liberal educations throw up a smoke screen of fake communication and the problems of rank and race become further repressed.

THE LANGUAGE OF RACISM

The mainstream in the United States assumes that the Northern European model of behavior is the optimum standard. People should be polite, confident and soft-spoken. They keep a lid on passion, power, sexuality and spirituality, split them off, and project them onto people they consider less educated or less evolved. These projections create a complex system of jealousy, anger and attraction.

The mainstream — in this case Northern white — communication style inadvertently presses minority groups into conforming. As a facilitator, you propagate racism if you support only one style of communication and behavior. Your staunch commitment to it is a political statement. You can be a neutral conflict-resolution negotiator only if you know the implicit, hierarchical assumptions in your own communication style. Encourage people to speak in the style that feels best to them, and if others cannot understand, find a translator.

ARE PEOPLE OUTSIDE THE UNITED STATES RACIST?

I remember a tense moment at a seminar in Slovakia in 1994. A Polish woman could not respond to the problems brought forward by American Blacks at the huge meeting. She insisted good-heartedly that all human beings were equal. A man from Germany agreed. There was no racism in Germany or Poland, they said. It took a long time for other people to make them realize racism existed in Poland and Germany as well as the United States.

People from mainstream groups in countries other than the United States often consider racism a uniquely American problem. Like Americans, Europeans forget history and the processes of colonization and imperialism. Perhaps that is why Central Europeans were so shocked when ethnic conflicts broke out in Eastern Europe after the demise of the Soviet republics.

It is not just people from the United States who are prejudiced; it is the mainstream everywhere. In Singapore, the Malaysians must battle the Chinese for survival. In Africa, Blacks fight white colonizers for freedom. Japanese mainstream people disavow their own indigenous people as well as migrant workers such as the Iranians and Koreans. In Australia, the white mainstream has practically annihilated the Aborigines. In German-speaking Switzerland, the Italians and Southern Mediterranean people are often treated like second-class citizens. Germany is seeing the rise of intolerance against darker-skinned foreigners, such as Turks, Africans and Tamil refugees. Gypsies are persecuted everywhere in Europe. Conservative, reactionary white Russians look down on the Azerbaijanis and Jews. Israelis look down on Palestinians and Arabs. In Northern Ireland, Protestants and Catholics, Irish and British are at war. Many cultures put down both Jews and Arabs, and everywhere, gays and lesbians are put down.

Who is not racist? The chilling truth is that we are all capable of bigotry. Blaming the whites in the West is an important step in working on the problem. But doing only that can also mask the tendency in the rest of the world to step on those perceived as lower. Since bigotry is only a symptom of a world problem, stopping it would not be a solution. Of course, the symptom must be treated by legislation before it kills. But the larger problem is the need for interconnectedness. Finally, it is everyone's task to bring awareness into our relationships.

PUTTING THE WORLD BACK IN ORDER

Indigenous people say that you are successful if your relationships are in order. By contrast, people in the West often say, "It is enough for me to change within my own heart and soul. Let others change as they need to. Don't push them."

In my view, if you only change yourself and take that to be more important than anything else you could do, you make a political statement to the effect that you are independent of other people, spirits, animals and the environment.

You may say: I love everybody. Let them develop on their own.

But I say: Your laissez-faire attitude is not tolerance. It is a form of self-indulgence. It is Eurocentric philosophy, Eastern passivity and plain middle class laziness. You appear to treat the world around you with compassion, but actually you erode your relationships with it by avoiding the discomforts of interaction. Your attitude puts up barriers between yourself and others. You secretly look down on them for not being as "developed" as you and for not growing as you think you are growing.

I say further: you kid yourself. If you loved others, you would say that everything around you is you, too. You may be liberal politically, but you segregate others from you when you avoid the trouble of relationships. You push those who are closest to you away and you keep the whole world at arm's length. How you use your power is not an individual matter; it is politics.

One virulent source of racism — the mainstream's alleged impotence to change the world — would disappear tomorrow if we realized that addressing conflicts and creating good relationships are keys to a meaningful life. Until you as a mainstream person address conflicts of rank and race, you must answer the question, "Who is racist?" with, "I am."

Part II

Revolution: Elders In The Fire

11

Singing About Troubled Waters

LOS ANGELES IN THE 1990S has been a metaphor for racial tension, like a pot of water heating on the stove. Although the city may look calm enough to outsiders, just one more degree of heat can send the water into a violent boil.

In April, 1965, the Watts riot left the city smoldering. Thirty-four Blacks died and more than a thousand were injured in one of the worst race riots the country has known. In April, 1992, violence erupted again following the acquittal of the four police officers accused of beating motorist Rodney King.

The Rodney King riot, in which fifty-six people were killed, sounded the alarm. Racism had not gone away. The deep-seated frustrations, inequity, poverty and hopelessness that racism breeds will not be assuaged by government programs or cosmetic surgery on inner cities. Today the pot of water is still on the verge of boiling: one degree from chaos, turbulence and rebellion. It would take only one blatant display of injustice to bring the violence back.

Some people see white capitalism at the root of racism. They believe that it creates drug lords and drug addicts and ruins the Black community. Some find the origins of racism in whites' historical imperialism against the Indians and Mexicans — an imperialism in the name of Christianity.

There are many proposals for addressing racism. Native Americans, Blacks, Japanese, Chinese and social activists from many other groups have suggestions, including improving economics, consciousness-raising, power-sharing, innerwork, strengthening relatedness, separatism, greater understanding of the overall situation, and revitalization of the family, church and community. Some of these directions promote greater integration and others forward separatism for disenfranchised groups.

THE LISTENER: A GHOST ROLE IN CONFLICTS

Worldwork integrates these approaches by allowing the issues to arise organically, even all together, at any meeting. I remember a conference on racism we gave in Oakland, California, that gives hope to those of us addressing racism.

Jean Gilbert Tucker, John Johnson, Max Schuepbach, Amy and I were among those from our process work community who acted as facilitators for a diverse group of about two hundred people. My book, *The Leader As Martial Artist*, had just come out, and *New Age Journal* asked Don Latin, a reporter from *The San Francisco Chronicle*, to come to the Oakland Conference. According to Latin's subsequent article:

> It had not been a good month in Oakland. The murder rate was rising in the Black community. A white cop confessed that he had strangled his wife and had tried to frame the city's street gangs by writing "war" on the side of her car. Oakland's mayor was on the verge of asking the military to help stop drive-by shootings. Crime had gotten out of hand. White residents of the Oakland Hills threatened to secede from the city and create their own town of "Tuscany."[1]

The local and national press were portraying Oakland as a war zone. Not many people wanted to come to Oakland for a racism conference. Only a week before the conference, we discovered that scarcely anyone had registered. Reading the papers, you got the sense that if you entered Oakland you would be shot on the spot.

At the last minute, the tide changed. This often happens with open city forums and seminars dealing with conflict. Most people are afraid and hope that at the last minute something will require them to go in another direction. Who wants trouble?

When we arrived at the conference site, Merrit College, the room was packed with Blacks, Latinos, whites, Japanese and Koreans. You could feel the tension in the air. It was the first seminar Amy and I had given in the United States where the police were in evidence. They came into the room whenever they thought the yelling was too loud.

My experience growing up in diverse groups helped me tolerate the tension. Even so, I found myself doing innerwork to rediscover my Asian, Latino and Black communication styles. I was aware that people would experience us not only through how we felt about them but through how we communicated.

The conference began on a Friday evening. Everyone seemed nervous and cautious. The next morning began quietly. Then a seemingly inconsequential demonstration set off an explosion. John Johnson and Max Schuepbach, an African American and a European American, were demonstrating a conflict-resolution procedure when a Black woman stood up and complained that the demonstration showed a white man putting down a Black man. She immediately went on and yelled that Black men put down Black women in the same way.

The quiet room went up in flames. Everyone was yelling at once. Our agenda to communicate training skills was taken over by conflict. Dealing with the situation scared many participants. Those who had come for a linear, cognitive presentation were upset too. "Where is the framework?" they demanded.

The situation left us no choice. We didn't know that it was only four days before what the press would call "the Rodney King race riots." The atmosphere was loaded. People began to vent their anger about racism and sexism. This was not like the quiet conversations of business meetings or the linear style of organizational development groups that the mainstream participants were accustomed to. It was a cacophony of themes, voices and pain.

In the midst of the chaos, a Black man spoke out with fury about the privilege of whites who give the good jobs to other whites while the Blacks get the undesirable jobs. Things escalated. A white man came forward to meet him, and the two men raged at each other, face to face, inches apart. The Black man screamed at the white man about his sense of supremacy and privilege, and the white man warned the Black that if he did not cool off and speak reasonably he would get his "ass kicked."

That did it. The fire roared. Privilege means, as the reader will realize by now, not only economic power, but the privilege of being cool, calm and detached in communication — the privilege of not having to listen to the rage, fury and sadness of those without power. The whites suddenly split apart; some tried to silence the white man, while others stood by to support him. Blacks came forward and rallied around the Black speaker.

As the voices rose to the screaming level, I remembered that people yell when no one is listening. The invisible, unrepresented part of the group, the ghost role, was the missing listener. I called out that I was listening to each speaker. I listened, and others in the audience began to chant "we are listening" as well. But there was another ghost role, too.

ANOTHER GHOST: SUFFERING

One after another, Black people of all ages, from high school students to elderly folks, came forward to speak about their fury and pain. Other Blacks yelled from the audience that they should stop emoting and let the whites do their work. You could almost taste the tension and agony.

Finally, a Black man came forward and began to sob, quietly, then more vehemently. He was crying out that his pain was the pain of everyone present. He suffered for everybody, and his suffering made some people listen. His heartfelt tears were meant to represent everyone's suffering from having been repressed and having repressed others for so long, from being unconscious of privileges and racism, from being unheard and unseen.

This man made the ineffable audible. The African American who had been arguing with the white man came forward to the center and hugged the weeping man. Slowly, Black women and men came to the center, surrounded him, and held the man as he sobbed. After a few minutes, white people and the rest of the audience came forward, and a huge human ball of warmth hugged that center of agony.

What had been missing in that conflict had been the genuine expression of suffering and pain. The roles of the various races had been represented, but not the role of suffering. It was a ghost.

HOPE AS A RESULT OF CONFLICT *in white community*

Nothing more needed to be done at that moment. The powerful experience that emerged from the pain brought people together. Many expressed hope; they felt this experience was reason enough to experiment with believing in humankind again.

After lunch, the conference continued. The large group gave its consent for the conflict in the white community to be the focus. A group of thirty white people came into the middle to work on racism with each other. One white man admitted that he did not want Black rage to force him to deal with anything; he did not like the implication that he had to change. Someone suggested that his attitude toward Blacks repressed them. He asked them to control their emotions to make it easy for him to listen. Wasn't this a misuse of mainstream privilege? Process workers pointed out that being cool was an option for someone living in a safe place. They argued that it was racist to want those who were being hurt to change their method of asking for change.

Other whites said they would never dream of changing. One white man rose in fury at another for being so arrogant. Amy facilitated the conflict. She pointed out that the accuser felt sad as well as angry and asked him to show it. He told the other man he could not, he felt so strongly about injustice. Why couldn't other whites get the point?

With Amy's help, the two men fought and, after about fifteen minutes, developed an understanding of one another. It turned out that the man who championed the status quo had never thought about racism before.

The white group continued to work on its conflicts. Many of the Blacks had never seen white people work on their racism, just as the whites had never seen Blacks work on themselves together. Very few people of either race had believed that a large group could enter into a process around race and survive, much less learn something.

Love Was The Bottom Line

On the final morning, people were in a great mood and applauded as one participant after another spoke: Blacks, Latinos, Japanese, gays and lesbians proudly described themselves. The group appreciated the differences. It was like a celebration. It had been a weekend to remember.

When the riots broke out in Los Angeles four days later, the city of Oakland, which had been among the very turbulent spots in the United States, was one of the few cities to remain calm. Riots incinerated neighboring San Francisco and other cities across the country. Oakland remained quiet. There wasn't a murder for 25 days following our seminar.

The San Francisco Chronicle reporter implied that the seminar was the reason for this calm. For me, the important thing was the hope that came from that incredible community process — those amazing speakers and leaders had demonstrated that a multicultural group could go so deeply into the unknown that they found within themselves love strong enough to create community.

Every Group Is Its Own Best Healer

Each group is its own expert on solving its conflicts. The Eurocentric style of conflict-management emphasizes procedures, compromise and solutions. It is weak in dealing with the emotional background of interpersonal conflict and relationships. The Eurocentric tradition values being on time and self-critical. African cultures are more relationship-oriented. Handling conflicts, each people needs its own psychology.

For example, according to Cecil Williams' book, *No Hiding Place*,[2] the Twelve Steps of Alcoholics Anonymous have not been able to help many Black clients. AA asserts that the Twelve Steps are the only way to become drug-free. This, Williams points out, sends a message to Blacks: "Nothing is missing from the Twelve Steps; something must be wrong with you."

He says further that AA contradicts African-American values. The Twelve Steps focus on individual recovery, whereas Blacks are communal people. A recovery program that focuses on the individual creates dissonance for people whose identity rests in belonging to an extended family and community. Moreover, Twelve Step programs pride themselves on anonymity. But

Black people have been invisible and unheard all their lives. For them, Williams says, anonymity is just more of the same, another way to remain faceless and be cut off from one another. Blacks need community that permits the expression of anger, rage, frustration, pain and failure.

I Am Because You Are

Williams continues, "Any community committed to healing must become a wailing wall or a screaming room."

Healing ourselves and our communities requires a healing hall, a community center, a wailing wall. The Western world, especially, needs such multicultural forums where feelings can be expressed, people can weep, people can rage, and where we can be channels for each other. If one person changes because of a deeply felt experience, everyone benefits. If people do not experience healing together, individual progress is inhibited.

We must recreate the world so we can be with one another. The majority of addicts have no world to go back to once they get clean or sober. Many of us are addicts in some way; we cling to something damaging that helps us get through our days — rank, for instance. We can work on rank within ourselves, but where do we go when we get clean from rank?

Our mainstream social system tries to hide trouble and pain. It represses the lessons that should have been learned from racism and history. The democratic world is addicted to peace and harmony; people in the mainstream use their rank and privilege to avoid conflict. The media spotlight individual speakers who represent conflicting interests, but the system inhibits large groups from coming together to work things out.

The mainstream lacks the indigenous wisdom that could heal it. We all suffer because we don't call on our African-American, Hispanic, Japanese, Chinese, Korean, Tibetan and European elders for help. We desperately need our Native American, African, Islamic, Jewish, Buddhist and Christian wisdom. We need every aspect of our diversity, including the disorder diversity brings with it, if we are to be whole.

Just as a person newly free of drugs needs a community that is clean, a community in recovery from racism needs a world that sees social inequities clearly. Right now, it doesn't exist.

In his lecture, "The Edge in Relationships," given at the Common Boundary Conference in Washington, DC, in 1992, John Johnson, an African-American teacher and process worker, stressed, like Cecil Williams, the importance of relationship in African-American psychology:

> In the African-American and African communities, relationships are the basis of all existence. They were there all along, and they are there after we leave. We are relationships.

> I am because you are. And you are because I am.... According to African-American philosophy, the spirit is our first relationship; it binds us together.... Each person is a spirit in themselves and it is the spirit behind all interactions.

The individual self cannot be differentiated from the community self; they are one spirit. Relationship-healing means getting to the bottom line, feeling that what we are experiencing belongs to community. It is the spirit moving us in unknown ways, making us afraid, angry and also peaceful.

Relationship means dealing with trouble, abuse, pain, fear and suffering. The Black singer, Bernice Johnson Reagon, told an audience at the Common Boundary Conference how deep relationships can develop out of trouble: "Through trouble, we find each other. I sing about trouble. Why is it that most folk talk about clear healing water while I sing about bloody, confused and turbulent waters?... Trouble brings us together."

Many of us hate to open the door when trouble knocks; we are afraid and only let in peace. But if we remember that, when trouble knocks, process is an unpredictable spirit trying to manifest, new relationships could begin. When trouble knocks, the possibility for a new kind of community is at the door. The new community is not based only on understanding one another, but on the common decision to enter into the unknown, into trouble — into that fire that is the price of liberty.

NOTES

1. "Mediators Target Hot Spots: They Let Angry Voices Cry Out, Calm the Rage," by Don Latin, *The San Francisco Chronicle*, Friday, May 1, 1992. His article in New Age Journal, September 1992, on the same topic was called, "Bridging the Gap."
2. Williams, *No Hiding Place*, p. 8.

12

Who's Got The Money?

SINCE ECONOMIC CLASS is a core issue behind social rank, a basic theme of organizations and communities everywhere is: "Who has the money?"

Since all issues are connected, one way or another, they all tie in with money. Education confers status, but education is expensive. People from lower economic classes have a harder time getting a good education. Unemployment and education are connected. Since poor people can't afford the training or education, the poor as a group experience the most unemployment. Mainstream races are paid more than others; white men are generally paid more than women.

The short-sighted mainstream says, "People who are unemployed must be lazy." Psychological damage enters the picture. Unemployed people internalize that criticism. Low self-worth leads to low resistance against disease. Poor health is tied to economic status — and so on.

Meanwhile, those who are well off say, "Look at all the programs for those people, and they still can't get their act together. The government doesn't make any program for me, but I got a job."

So-called "affirmative action" programs that favor hiring those who are kept down in the economic system cannot achieve equality of employment because such programs do not deal with background prejudice. That, in turn, leads to frustration for the economically disadvantaged, who were promised a better life. Some of those people will buy into the mainstream view that there must be something wrong with them. Their low self-esteem leads to poor health, and with poor health they cannot easily work. Family tension results. Children are neglected.

Race, gender, health, education and money are linked and produce higher rank for some and powerlessness for others.

THE NEXT REVOLUTION IS TOMORROW

The world is ripe for a new form of communism to bring about class equality. I predict a revolution in our general awareness of rank that will cut across all social issues. In the absence of education to create awareness of rank, I believe that riots and revolt to achieve this revolution are inevitable. I would like to be wrong.

By communism, I mean the process of equalizing class. Communism is not only an historical episode that we have witnessed in such countries as China, Vietnam, Cuba, and, until recently, Russia. Communism is a phase in community process trying to happen wherever a conflict arises between those who have money and those who don't.

I base my prediction of revolution on my experience with multicultural groups in near-riot situations around the world, and on the observation that any group process, regardless of the country or organization, is connected to the world's unsolved problems. That is, group process is connected with issues of gender, race, health, money and social class, and with unconsciousness of rank.

Is my prediction of revolution Marxist? Yes and no. Marx's predictions of revolt were based only on economic considerations. As I have indicated, economic conditions are not independent of other problems. I make my prediction after looking at the entire spectrum.

We repeat history. Even small-town political processes repeat the history of recent world revolutions, whether or not the people involved know this history. There will always be new variations on the Bolshevik rebellion against a selfish, greedy monarchy. And there will be new leaders like Joan of Arc, Gandhi, Malcolm X and Martin Luther King, Jr., as long as there are new variations on religious oppression and racism.

It is crucial for those of us working on group processes to see our job in the larger context of human history. Even if a town must deal with a conflict as mundane as a proposal to raise money to strengthen an old bridge, the problem is connected to world history. The bridge may be a hot item because, let's say, there's a lot of unemployment in the town, and people need work. But, on the other hand, the bridge is not falling down yet, and the rich don't want to pay higher taxes to get money to rebuild the bridge. It comes down to: who has the money and who doesn't? If the rich win, the ground is prepared for minor-scale class revolution.

In biology, it's said that "ontogeny recapitulates phylogeny." In other words, the development of the individual human being from conception in the womb to adulthood (ontogeny), mirrors the historical development of the entire species of human beings (phylogeny). For instance, the human embryo grows a tail, which it drops before birth. In the same way, like early humans, groups of us huddle together in communities for friendship and safety. Tensions develop, power struggles arise, somebody with charisma seizes leadership, friends of the leader are accorded high rank, slaves or immigrants have low rank. Conflicts arise over diversity, race, gender, health, community, equality, democracy, indigenous spirituality, capitalism, communism and finally deep democracy.

Any group you can think of — a business, a religious congregation, a town hall meeting or a bridge club — repeats history. Any given group will go through some of the following:

- A time when spiritual experience, new ideas or outer danger bring people together.
- A dictatorial phase, when someone takes over and tells the rest of us what to do.
- A struggle for consensus on what to do next.
- An experiment with democracy — an attempt to secure rights and give everyone equal power.

- A period of imperialistic take-over when the group tacitly agrees that it's time to expand regardless of what is pushed back.
- A period of retaliation from other groups.
- Resulting battles over territory, against people and the environment. The environment rebels.

I would love to add another phase to this list. Though it has not occurred yet, as far as I know, it nevertheless seems inevitable:

- A time of greater awareness and deep democracy to deal with age, race, religion, gender, health or sexual-orientation conflicts and the problems of the environment.

GHOSTS: THE FORCES CALLED SOCIETY

At any moment, in any phase of a group process, there are hundreds of roles: the practical person, the emotional person, the child, the wise woman, the courageous soldier and many, many more. They all have to co-exist. Until now, people under both democratic and dictatorial governments have lived with three forces:

The Spiritual Leader, who connects us to the infinite. In recent times, this role has been filled by someone whose actions are based more on visions than on practicalities.

The Dictator, a leader who uses power excessively and abusively.

The Social Activist, who opposes oppression by becoming a freedom fighter and later a revolutionary.

These timespirits take on great importance in times of crisis. There are hundreds of variations on these ghosts. The names are not important; it is their existence and energy we must notice. Moreover, it is crucial to remember that each of us is in one role or another at any given time. We don't necessarily stay in the same role. Despite role-shifting, community endures.

Process. The fourth timespirit is process. When the other roles are brought together, process transcends them and forges them into community. The Process cements the other roles into community through conflict, discussion and dialogue.

Take your own extended family as examples. Someone in the role of the dictator habitually takes a stand without asking others if it's okay. If the dictator goes too far, the social activist speaks up and says: "We have not reached consensus. Don't tread on others. This is my area, not yours. Stay in your own area." Then someone becomes a spiritual leader, governed by visions, dreams and sudden intuitions, and pulls people together again.

IF COMMUNISM DIDN'T EXIST, IT WOULD HAVE TO BE INVENTED

History of Economics

Since every multicultural group reenacts the social issues of history, facilitators must have insight into the history of economics and human rights in order to understand group processes and predict where they are going.

Take the case of communism. If it didn't exist, it would have to be invented. Communism, in its attempt to distribute wealth and work to the economically disempowered, is the inevitable reaction to capitalism. It aims to correct the myopia that ignores the dependence of economic privilege on class, race, sex, age, education and other intangible resources.

Karl Marx, the parent of Communism, believed that societies progress from slave ownership to feudal conditions to capitalism to socialism and finally to a utopian communist society. He saw Europe of the nineteenth century as a sleeping giant, a mass of slumbering people subjugated by a few.

He recognized that people who have capital don't need to sell their labor to survive. These constitute the class called the bourgeoisie. If you have no capital, you must sell your labor to stay alive, and you belong to the proletariat. Capitalism is the dialectic (opposition) between the bourgeoisie and the proletariat. If the economic basis of society were changed, Marx thought, culture would in time change too. If people abandoned their faith in private ownership, the conflict between the interests of the few and the needs of the masses would disappear.

In worldwork terms, Marx thought as a social activist. He said that getting rid of rank, the greedy monarch and the dictator and following the vision of class equality would bring us heaven on earth, that is, society without class differences. But we know from history that no one has succeeded in getting rid of the ghosts. At best, we can use them to make community.

LENIN'S REVOLUTION: AN EXPEDIENT DICTATORSHIP

This insight is easy to come by today. But the poverty in which Lenin and others lived forced them to revolt. Lenin modified Marx's ideas of the 1840s and 1850s to fit the conditions of Russia at the beginning of the twentieth century, when the small ruling class had extreme wealth and the landless peasants suffered extreme poverty. Lenin, more radical than Marx, believed that individuals who wanted to be richer than others must be overcome by force; he didn't agree with sitting around and letting the conflict between the have's and have-not's play itself out. Marx had written that the oppressed would gain power slowly, but Lenin was determined to shorten the transition. He and his associates organized and inspired the famous October 1917 Bolshevik Revolution.

Seizing power in the name of the workers, the Bolsheviks put an end to Romanoff rule and its imperial culture. Within weeks, land, property and industry became state-owned. With this one move, to the stupefaction of the rest of the world, the people of more than one-sixth of the globe were politically reorganized by a communist regime.

In its haste, the Leninist movement went further than it had promised; it went beyond sharing power. The workers created a new oppressive party and recreated a ruling class that sacrificed the utopian dream of communism for a dictatorship that could get things moving. The revolutionaries switched roles, almost without realizing it at first. Where recently there had been an autocratic monarchy, now there was the Communist Party, a new form of totalitarianism. It forbade essential freedoms such as freedom of speech, freedom to congregate and freedom of worship. By 1930, the first planned central economy had come into being. In a clandestine way, it gave more power and money to some and less to others. The people of Russia again knew oppression.

POLITICAL CORRECTNESS AND THE DEMISE OF THE USSR

The communist movement was soon dominated by an ideology. The Party insisted on political correctness. Bogna Szymkiewicz, a Polish woman I met in Warsaw, explained the psychological consequences of being under communist rule:

The Poles call this condition "Polish Schizophrenia." In my thoughts, I felt free. The problem was a huge discrepancy between the world of thought and the world of action. And somewhere, very deeply, I was sure that nothing could be done against the regime.

In my inner world, everything was possible. You could be as creative as you wanted. Outside, the situation was too dangerous to interfere with.

The outer situation had been increasing in danger since the onset of the revolution. Lenin died in 1924 at the age of 54. James Defronzo points out in his *Revolutions and Revolutionary Movements* that, had Lenin lived, he might have loosened up to become more democratic; his rigidity was caused by the problems of the revolution itself. He was succeeded by Stalin, popularly called "The Iron Man," whose incompetence became clear only after he was entrenched in power. He was brutal in his repression of his opponents.

Marx, Lenin, Trotsky, Mao and others were the heroes of people who had been severely exploited by monarchs or landlords. Communist ideas fell upon fertile soil in China, where the great majority of people lived as feudal vassals with no social power or property. Like Russia, China was slow to enter the industrial era, which increased its poverty relative to Western nations.

Fired by democratic ideals, communism tried to lead Russia and China into the industrial period and modern times. But even under the iron hand of Stalin, Russia never quite pulled out of its economic difficulties. Later, the Soviet Union's attempt to keep step with the development of nuclear weapons by the United States diverted enormous amounts of money from its internal needs, making the people more frustrated than ever. Finally, the cloak of dictatorship repressed new and creative ideas and led to rigidification. The rest is history.

At the end of the 1980s, under the influence of *glasnost* and Gorbachev's relaxation of restrictions, the Soviet Union crumbled. Encouraged by the success of the Solidarity Party in Poland, other Eastern European countries broke away from Soviet rule. However, the lesson of rigidity and the oppression that results from it had not yet been learned.

A History Lesson: Don't Forget Revenge

Marx and his followers realized that much of world history orbits around those with money. The communists hoped to establish a utopia in which everyone would work for everyone else without egotism. But Lenin was naive when he proclaimed that national problems are resolved only by force. The force of revolution that he hoped would be temporary in the end became tradition.

He understood that driven by despair, people would be willing to use any means to end hunger. He believed that the basis of socialism was finding bread. But soon the revolution looked to find revenge for the workers' not having had bread. The communists not only removed the monarchs, they cut off their heads.[1]

Today, if the democratic reforms in the countries of the former Soviet Union do not succeed in bettering life, the ground is prepared for another bloody revolution. Communist ideals must return because those countries still need an egalitarian distribution of privilege and security. Already as I write, in 1995, Communists are being elected to local government positions in cities of the former Eastern Block.

What can we learn from history? Depression, despair and poverty make people desperate. They will try almost anything to survive. They will follow almost anyone who promises immediate relief. At first it's a matter of life and death. Once revenge becomes the motive, they get drunk on the very power they needed to save themselves. They become the slave-masters they wanted to overcome. When you project the outcome of a group process, don't forget the force of revenge.

Visions Turning Into Their Opposites

As this historical view of communism has demonstrated, the most wonderful democratic visions easily turn into new forms of dictatorship. Domination by the new "ideals" has the same effect as public abuse everywhere: people are devastated.

At one of my recent lectures about the former Soviet Union, two women, Luba Ivanova-Surkin from Moscow and Alina Wrona from Gdansk, Poland, spoke of their experiences under communist dictatorships. Alina told us that communism is much more than not being allowed freedom of speech. It is not even being allowed to think:

It is more than you can even imagine. If you do not agree with others, you will be fired from work and lose everything you own. From this lack of freedom you develop an inner censor and you change. You shut off so you cannot think. The official outer censors are also inside your mind. It is what we called in Poland the "inner immigration police." It is so scary to think your own thoughts, you do not dare.

My first impression when I came to the United States was how much freedom you have here. It is incredible how much. You can go out and say, "I don't agree!" or "I don't like it!" I am amazed at how you can talk, even on TV, against laws!

Luba Ivanova-Surkin, who grew up in Moscow and escaped before the revolution of 1989, said that in Russia, people had to:

... just be quiet, keep your feelings and your thoughts — if you have any — inside! That is the safest place for them to be. Actually, it is better if you don't have any feelings. They might threaten your everyday existence. Don't you dare speak! It is too dangerous.... But after learning how to swim with the current, you learn to go against the current and change from being quiet and peaceful to outrageous and powerful. Whenever you are oppressed, you stay "inside" to protect yourself. To exist, you must appear to swim with the current. Going against the current is most difficult when your entire world is ruled by a totalitarian government. Either you become outrageous and are attacked or you suffocate internally.

Compare the inner experiences of women living in communist countries to those of Bernice Johnson Reagon, an African-American singer who was born in the United States:

I grew up in a culture of struggle where, without any specific spoken warning, I received clear messages of boundaries in all aspects of my life that were not to be crossed, rules that were not to be broken. I internalized these messages, thus setting up a central mechanism to protect myself against acting freely. I went around in life with this inner warning light or buzzer that would be triggered if I considered an action that was considered inappropriate behavior. There was a tape in my head that chanted, "If you do that you are going to be killed."... I am talking about a fear of being shut out, cut off if you behaved in unacceptable ways. Within the home, the school, and the church, you had a

sense that this structure of boundaries were set up by people who cared about you and wanted you to do well.[2]

History repeats itself. Communism, which planned to overcome monarchy, created a totalitarian regime. Democracy in the
United States, which aimed to overcome rulership by one class,
made new feudal boundaries to keep certain people down. This
is why social activists and facilitators must make awareness their
first priority. Don't overlook social rank or the spiritual rank that
fuels revenge.

The Death Of The World

How did Bernice Johnson Reagon overcome her sense of inner
oppression?

> Today... I operate out of the assumption that I am the United
> States of America and that I am central to anything that is
> really happening in this country that is worthwhile. I recog-
> nize that I am a secret. Our [Black] history, our contribu-
> tions, and our culture are important.... We are presented as
> being subcultural, as if we are outside the other — a tangent
> or a limb that if lost by the main body, life would not be
> threatened.[3]

U.S. mainstream culture made her feel like a superfluous
limb. If you are in the white mainstream, you may claim that life
in a democracy cannot be compared to life under a dictatorship.
The thought is shocking. Yet, psychologically, the effect of
oppression is the same. Democratic societies without awareness
finally create the same inner experience as dictatorships. Individuals from marginalized communities must obey, or their lives are
worthless.

Bernice Johnson Reagon survived by realizing that she is the
world, and without her and all African Americans, the world will
die. Likewise, the atmosphere in the global community dies if
any part of it is cut off. The world cannot survive spiritually without the indigenous people, the Black community, every community and every individual. Sustainable community — that is,
deep democracy — dies if anyone's viewpoint, story or ideas are
negated. Many of us feel that the world has died many times
because this negation happens so often.

Take A Look At Your Visions

Utopian visions replace tyranny with tyranny, or drive its forces underground. No one has ever succeeded in dominating domination. No vision or government can succeed unless we are aware of fear, rank, oppression, power and abuse by outer and internalized officials.

Try out the following questions on your ideals and visions:

1. What kind of organizations do you prefer to support? Think about one of these organizations.

2. What vision does this group profess? What beliefs do these visions try to change?

3. Who are the real or imagined opponents of your group? What kinds of people or events is the vision trying to overcome? How will those events and the people be dealt with according to your group's vision?

4. How does your group work with conflicting opinions? Imagine a group process in which you bring up opposite viewpoints to the group's vision. How will your group react? How would you prefer to see conflict resolved?

5. Consider inviting your group to set up a position for each differing viewpoint in the field and process their interaction.

6. Go through these questions again, using the term "myself" instead of "my group." What is one of your favorite visions in life? What part of you does not agree with this vision? How do you deal with this part of yourself?

Deep democracy depends upon facilitating interactions between visionaries and "non-believers." Without democracy, a group is unsustainable, because it is eventually weakened and destroyed by the timespirit of the non-believers who are always present, not only in the generic field, but in each of us. History teaches that facilitating issues around a group's vision is the most crucial thing you can do.

Hypnotized By Ideals

When Amy and I visited Berlin and Moscow in the early 1990s, both cities suffered from poverty and crippled economies in the aftermath of Soviet domination. Everyone was in pain. People looked for scapegoats. In Eastern Germany, the secret police were blamed. In Moscow's Red Square, loudspeakers blared that Jews had created Russia's financial problems.

We found that many people still loved communism; others hated it. In Moscow, "comrades" sat at their desks in front of public doorways to institutes and research centers, grimly asking for identification, as if the Soviets were still in power.

In the meetings we facilitated, we experienced hundreds of highly sensitive and intelligent people searching for information about themselves. They were desperate to learn about psychology and about the world outside. In the wake of Soviet dictatorship, people were afraid to talk about personal needs. They also had a sense of inferiority due to the failure of their governments. Nevertheless, pride in communist ideas lingered on.

During our stay in Berlin, we took part in a meeting between "Ossies" and "Wessies," Germans from the former Eastern German Democratic Republic and West Germans. When the Wall fell, it left the communists and capitalists facing one another with problems that had not been worked out. History had erected not only a cement wall, but a psychological barrier of doubt and pain.

In a large group where people from both sides met for the first time, a West German man got up and accused the East Germans of having been morally weak in accepting the communists. "Why did you bow down to them?" he demanded in a righteous tone.

An East German woman stood up and said, with poise, "But you have been morally weak. The ideals of the West have died. Money and flashy cars and big buildings are not ideals. You have become materialists without ethics."

The discussion became intense, as both sides continued making accusations and also spoke of hopes that hadn't been fulfilled. Suddenly a man from the East German side went over the edge. He revealed the pain of living under "Stasi," the East German secret police. Everyone seemed to freeze.

We stayed with the hot spot, and after some hesitation and trepidation, another East German admitted that the original ideals of communism were more attractive than anything he had ever come across. Ideals, they were the problem! Suddenly there were no longer two sides, but one group describing the hypnotic effect of visions and ideals. A West German woman spoke passionately about how she had been blind to the cruelty of a guru whose brutal actions towards people were overlooked because of the religious convictions he preached. Others shared their experiences. The process ended with an unanswered question that united us:

Why do we believe in great visions and overlook the power visionaries have to coerce us? Perhaps all visions, regardless of their value, inspire us and also blind us to what's involved in carrying them out.

THE BASIC DIALECTIC: GREED VERSUS LOVE

History shows us that we cannot succeed in repressing our greed, our drive to dominate the earth or our will to become rulers. Marxism and Leninism have not eradicated these tendencies from the human character; they only repressed them. Communism has been no more successful in wiping out self-centeredness than the West has been in suppressing evil. Democracy cannot be achieved if it does not become deeper, if we do not notice and bring forward and process our egotism, greed and hunger for power. If we merely inhibit them, we recapitulate the origins of every revolution throughout history.

The startling message is: respect egotism, bring it out. At the same time, honor our love for one another. Let the great forces meet. Let these two timespirits enter into a process with one another. We need a gathering of representatives of the values of the past and spokespeople for the values for the future, for idealism and fatalism, leadership and terrorism, love and greed.

Let's bring the bigotry and community, greed and love forward and sit with them in the fire. Culture need not be hindered by egotism, prejudice, fatalism and greed. If we bring them out and get into them, we can move beyond. The dialectic between the timespirits of greed and love will consistently bring us something new and unexpected. This new thing is community.

RELIGION: MANY PEOPLE'S DRUG OF CHOICE

Revolution follows economic necessity. Marx saw that the proletariat is easily drugged by favors from those in power. Those favors usually involve property.

Were he alive today, he'd point out our government's rewards for not rocking the boat: you are allowed, for instance, a place to live, a VCR and a car of your own. These perks drug you, and in your drugged condition you are oblivious to your government's glaring inadequacies.

When our basic economic needs are met, when we have the comfort of our own apartment and a TV, we tend to ignore social problems. We forget privilege and rank as soon as we have them. When we enjoy enough food to satisfy hunger and enough material things to keep us from being bored, we are less likely to trouble the government about imperialist policies.

Marx said that people use religion like drugs: "Religion is the opiate of the people." In our culture today, there's plenty to support his position. Many psychological and spiritual groups avoid politics. They prefer to meditate, work on their dreams, recreate old rituals, and focus on their relationship to a deity, the unconscious or their lover. They don't want to be embroiled in social change. They are interested in the innerwork that leads to the integrated person, harmony and peace, but not the worldwork in which we have to tolerate conflict. They create "community process" that forbids anger, saves the forests or the spotted owls, while remaining uninformed about the effects of toxic wastes in the inner city or the experience of AIDS.

MEANING IS TO SPIRIT WHAT FOOD IS TO THE BODY

Marx and Lenin did not foresee, however, the depression that results from their non-psychological, anti-religious doctrines. They stressed community but negated the dreamfield in which we live. They hoped for a classless family but forbade the community of humans and spirits to which all human beings are indigenous.

Certainly, they were right: when people have been underprivileged, abused and poor, the drive for money can make them dizzy and vengeful. The greater the differential between wealth and poverty in the society, the more intense the anger or more profound the despair of the poor. But Marx and Lenin were also wrong: a connection to the gods is power that allows you to transcend despair.

Governments that try to forbid this connection end up depressing the individual's sense of meaning, which is independent of time. This meaning is finally as necessary and important as food.

Communism is like capitalism; both are Western, European and materialistic in the sense of forwarding property ownership, whether by the few or by the masses. Both devalue aesthetic and intellectual experience that are not related to the economy. Both negate the environment. Both ignore the spiritual and mystic traditions of indigenous peoples, whose spirituality is based on connectedness to all beings.

The Oglala Lakota patriot, Russell Means, contrasted Marxism with Native American beliefs and spiritual traditions:

> A lopsided emphasis on humans by humans, the European arrogance of acting as though they were beyond the nature of all related things, can only result in a total disharmony and a readjustment which cuts arrogant humans down to size, gives them a taste of that reality beyond their grasp or control.... There is no need for a revolutionary theory to bring this about. It's beyond human control.[4]

The paradox of group process is this: to be useful, it must address everyone's social and rank issues. It's got to deal with the issue of who has the money. At the same time, a community dies if it focuses on only what is right or wrong about each side. As Russell Means stated, community is doomed too if its only concern is people. The bottom line is the spirit of nature, the mysterious fiery process which propels us into and through all the different aspects of ourselves and the roles in our community.

NOTES

1. See the works of Marx, Lenin, Trotsky, Luxemburg and Mao in the Bibliography for more details on history.
2. Bernice Johnson Reagon, in her Foreword to *Reimaging America: The Arts of Social Change*, eds. Mark O'Brien and Craig Little.
3. Ibid.
4. An article titled "Marxism is a European Tradition" in *Akwesasne Notes*, Summer 1980, p. 17ff.

13

The Metaskills Of Elders

ELDERS HAVE MORE than leaders' abilities. Amy calls the special feeling skills and attitudes needed to be of service to others "metaskills."[1]

Until now, you may have expected yourself to be a strong leader, a good teacher, parent, organizational development specialist or politician. Or perhaps you've been a strategist, planning, calculating and logically analyzing ways to change cities and the world, or a military leader who thinks of power first instead of awareness. Deep down, though, you may suspect that all the planning, analyzing, and structuring in the world will never be enough.

You may have a hunch that an entirely different level of skills is needed. Perhaps you've felt that you have the potential for such skills. Perhaps you suspect you have powers that would apply not only to personal life, but in a larger arena as well.

It is most important to find your style of eldership, the one which works with your communities. Will you become the kind of elder who stands powerfully? Can you also let things be? There is a time to rush, and a time to do nothing.

- The leader follows *Robert's Rules of Order*; the elder obeys the spirit.
- The leader seeks a majority; the elder stands for everyone.
- The leader sees trouble and tries to stop it; the elder sees the troublemaker as a possible teacher.
- The leader strives to be honest; the elder tries to show the truth in everything.
- The democratic leader supports democracy; the elder does this, too, but also listens to dictators and ghosts.
- Leaders try to be better at their jobs; elders try to get others to become elders.
- Leaders try to be wise; elders have no minds of their own. They follow the events of nature.
- The leader needs time to reflect; the elder takes only a moment to notice what's happening.
- The leader knows; the elder learns.
- The leader tries to act; the elder lets things be.
- The leader needs a strategy; the elder studies the moment.
- The leader follows a plan; the elder honors the direction of a mysterious and unknown river.

Learn To Learn

With a small team that included a trainee, I once facilitated a large group meeting for an organization that was having serious economic trouble. Our male trainee and a female middle manager from the organization got into a conflict that seemed, at first, to have nothing to do with the organization's problems. Our trainee complained to the middle manager, "Every time I open my mouth, you get angry with me."

The woman responded, "That's all in your head."

The trainee took a deep breath and suggested they work on their conflict in the center. "Who knows?" he said. "This might be useful for others as well." After some hesitation, she agreed. The two went to the center of the circle.

"The first step for me, as a conflict advisor, is to listen. Please speak," he said to her.

She seemed fired up. "In my opinion, there are a lot of conflicts in this organization. You and the rest of your team, including Amy and Arny, were hired to solve them. You should take more of a stand and create resolutions rather than waiting for people to resolve things themselves!" By now she was red in the face. She said vehemently, "I expect you to model peace-making!"

He started shaking and responded defensively, "If I resolved things, you and others might not learn how to do it yourselves. Besides, the issues that were coming forward couldn't be resolved at that very moment." He recommended that the organization sit with the tensions and not avoid them.

The woman disagreed completely. "You have to model what you know about resolution and stop following some method. How else can we learn?"

She convinced him. He thanked her. Right away, he became less passive and more dynamic. "Okay," he said, "since you have become my teacher, my first job is to take a firm hand. I am now going to resolve the discord between the two of us!"

She grinned at his decisiveness. Simultaneously, she looked strangely sad. He said, "You are smiling, but I see an expression I can't identify in your eyes. What are you feeling?"

"Nothing much," she said. She began to cry. After a few minutes, she said, "I am touched that you have chosen me to work with in the center of the circle. No one appreciates me in this organization."

Everyone was shocked at her words. Our trainee stuttered; he did not know what to say. He tried to apologize for himself and others who had not paid enough attention to her ideas. He told her he was thankful that she had encouraged him to be more himself. This, he said, had always been a problem for him. He decided that in the future, instead of sitting back encouraging others, he would be more active himself. They both wept together.

What a scene! One of the organization's top managers said he had never seen anything like this. A middle manager, who was a woman, said, "Right on! That's been the problem around here all along; no one shows any feeling. We should all learn from her."

The room became quiet. After a while, people began to express their deepest feelings, shyly at first, then more openly. Once various kinds of deep emotions and feelings were in the open, people spontaneously worked together on the organization's financial problems. Within an hour, management and employees worked together and came up with a method to solve their financial crisis: be more feeling with customers.

Of the metaskills used by our trainee, the most important was seeing the woman as his teacher and becoming a student of that process.

DREAMING OUR WAY FROM DEMOCRACY TO DEEP DEMOCRACY

As an elder, you must be constantly aware of which timespirits are having their say and which are not. Your awareness metaskills help you feel certain things, clarify power and sense feelings that can barely be verbalized. Listen, not only to vengefulness and threats of terrorism, but to transcendent visions and ineffable longing. Many people have powerful inner experiences they don't know how to express. Not everything can be said; some messages can only be heard in prayer; others have to be sung, danced or manifested in silence. An elder puts unconscious, dream-like and transpersonal states at the group's service.

Wherever we come together, what indigenous people call the "dreaming process" is present. In this altered state of consciousness, fantasies, intuitions and insights can be noticed right alongside today's problems. When these are expressed in words, dance or song, the atmosphere changes and amazing solutions appear.

The more sensitive you are to the social atmosphere, the more sensitive you are likely to be to the dreaming process. In the groups you will facilitate, there will be people who have been overlooked in decision-making and other processes because they seemed too quiet, too irritating, too strange, too full of fantasies, seemed to have their own language or to live in their own world. They may have been, in effect, banished from the group because they were rebels, mystics, psychics or mediums; they are furious or otherworldly. They may have done time in jail or a facility for "the mentally ill." They may have been treated in a humiliating way, tied to a doctor's couch. Their relatives may have discounted them.

You, as an elder, may recognize that these individuals are potential teachers. By respecting them, you will help the rest of the group learn to value dreams and rely on the voices in the wind to point out the next steps.

To move from democracy to deep democracy, we need only to ask:

Who is noticing something interesting?
What does it feel like here?
Who is dreaming something they can barely notice?
What does the spirit of the earth say now?
What other spirits are present?
What are you feeling?
Who is comfortable? Who is uncomfortable?

We need the freedom to dream at all times and especially during group processes. Deep democracy means that everyone must be encouraged to note and express whatever they are feeling. It means that everyone gives internal permission for these altered states to occur. Just as in deep democracy, we give attention to overt and covert social issues and the people who have been marginalized, so we must give attention to the states of consciousness we have marginalized because they were unfamiliar. We must ask what those states of consciousness have to say. World change can begin with dreams.

follow the unknown

LET IT BE

While leaders make strategies to win, the elder recognizes others and becomes their student. The leader focuses on the issues; the elder, on feelings as well. The leader tries to change people; the elder assumes we are all exactly what we are meant to be. The leader thinks the future depends on which political party heads the government; for an elder, the future depends on enabling what is unknown to appear. Therefore the elder focuses upon interactions between the visible and hidden polarities, not on the domination or success of any one of them.

When a deep-seated social conflict has been expressed, when each party has taken a side and the issues are clear, an elder lets the process be — even if there is no resolution. Accepting the lack of closure can be a relief to people. At times, of course, you will feel you must take the lead. Still, if you model being a follower of the unknown, if you sense that life is up to powers greater than you, people in the group you are facilitating will also learn this awareness and respect.

In a seminar I once facilitated, a violent conflict erupted between a Black woman and a white woman. The Black woman screamed in the face of the white woman, "You think about your-self all the time and do not see that by focusing on your troubles, you neglect mine! You're being racist."

The white woman responded, "I am not racist. You are too damn pushy."

The two women faced each other and had it out. They yelled. They moved toward each other and backed off. They yelled some more. There was no resolution. They disagreed. I saw their dou-ble signals of turning away from each other, so I recommended they let go and wait for the next day. "Turn away," I said. "That's the process for the moment." Because the double signals repre-sented their real feelings, they could let go and drop the issue for the moment.

The next morning, the white woman said she had dreamed of a yogi who sat near an open door. She felt enlightened and said to the Black woman, "When I woke up, I understood that you were saying white people focus on their own agony and do not see that doing this closes the door to the rest of the world. I am sorry I did not have the detachment yesterday to understand this." The Black woman was very touched.

An elder watches double signals, follows nature and lets it be. Nature has its own way of solving things

THE TAO AND THE ELDER

At the beginning of this book, I said that I had developed process work from Jungian insights and Taoism. Worldwork later devel-oped from process work. The *Tao Te Ching,* one of the oldest books on earth, discusses many of the abilities necessary to facili-tate groups and get along with people and nature.

Recorded around 600 B.C. in pre-Confucian China, the *Tao Te Ching* is about following nature in everyday life. Its legendary author, Lao Tse, recommended following the moment rather than a preconceived program. One of his goals was learning to lose. This may sound absurd to contemporary leaders or organi-zational development experts, but it is a profound insight for working with groups in conflict. Since the chapters of the *Tao Te Ching* are untitled, I call Chapter 48 "The Winning Loser."

The Winning Loser 48

The student of knowledge [aims at] learning
    day by day.
The student of Tao [aims at] losing day by day.

By continual losing,
One reaches doing nothing.
By doing nothing, everything is done.

He who conquers the world often does so
    by doing nothing.
When one is compelled to do something,
    the world is already beyond
    his conquering.[2]

The ancient Chinese concept of the elder or sage reverses our conventional Western ideas of leadership. While our leaders gather information to find out what to do next, that is, "learn day-by-day," sages notice how irrelevant "expert" knowledge can be to the reality of the moment. They realize that they cannot push events or the human species further than it can go just now. Nature teaches them to be losers, wait and do nothing but become aware.

As a worldwork elder, you have to wait and follow environmental and human signals, dreams, the body signals, the wind, the trees, the direction of nature. Otherwise, you will model the attempt at domination that is responsible for so many of our personal and world problems.

Doing nothing does not necessarily mean being totally passive. It means not pushing, following what is present and using the energy of what is happening instead of forcing things. At first, it is natural to push and try to force things to happen your way. Then, if things do not go your way, if nature does not support you, try questioning it. Test it, see if you are at an edge, and try again. Try a couple of times, and if it does not move in your direction, let go.

The pusher must learn to lose. Nature has the power, and the only intervention that works is one that follows the whole group process. Ancient wisdom tells us that the leader in you is dangerous. It hopes to do what you planned. This causes you to ignore the experiences people are having in the moment. Learn to have a leader's ego and then learn to drop it. Remember death; very few of us live forever. Learn from death to drop yourself, your plan and strategy after you have tried it. Then you win, even when you lose.

WATER 水

To work with people, the Tao Te Ching recommends we develop metaskills that are like the qualities of water: freedom and benevolence. This is from Chapter 8:

> *Benevolence* supreme good
>
> The highest benevolence is like water.
> The benevolence of water is to benefit all
>   beings without strife.
> It dwells in places which man despises,
>   therefore it stands close to Tao.
>
>   ... In giving, benevolence shows itself in love.
>   ... In speech, benevolence shows itself in truth.[3]

How can water be benevolent? Water goes everywhere it can without fighting. It just flows and waits to find the lowest spot. You and I, on the other hand, usually stop when we get into scary areas, those lower, unknown places. The benevolence of water is not to judge, but to flow on, even where others dread to go.

Change and transformation arise out of such places. As a benevolent elder, just by being who you are, by saying uncanny things, by doing outrageous acts, by modeling the freedom and compassion of water, you enable other people to venture into places they've never before been. Imagine yourself weeping in public, speaking personally, laughing at yourself, meditating in public, playing like a child, rolling on the floor. See yourself as forceful, also as passive.

You facilitate nature in whatever communication nature wishes to make — uninhibited by what "should" or "should not" be said or done in public. As a person, you respect social issues and people. As water, you do or say just about anything that comes into your head.

An elder is a channel for information pouring from the vast potential of nature into the moment in everyday life. Your metaskills allow you to say the lowest, most gruesome things and the highest, most spiritual as well. As an elder, let "impossible" things happen.

World elders enable communication by encouraging themselves and others to go over their edges, to flow over boundaries that separate us. Sometimes people from disavowed viewpoints must be forceful and take over a group to get their point across. While they issue ultimatums and threaten the group, ask yourself what water feels when it is coerced or threatened. Water does not get insulted. Water doesn't rear up and say, "How dare you talk to me like that?" Water remains water, it responds, it flows up against the rocks, crashing, then melts around them. Water envelops its opponent, or retreats if the other gets too high.

WIND 5

Chapter 5 of the ancient text talks about the metaskill I call "Cosmic Breath."

Cosmic Breath

Heaven and earth are not humane;
They treat the ten thousand beings as
 straw dogs.
The sage is not human;
He treats the hundred families as straw dogs.

Between heaven and earth how like a bellows the
 Tao is, empty and yet inexhaustible.
Moving and yet it pours out ever more.
By many words, one's reckoning is exhausted.
It is better to abide by the center.[4]

"Not humane" here does not mean cruel; it means nature in contrast to culture. "Inhuman" refers to dreaming — our ability to detach, to behave in countercultural, non-hierarchical ways.[5]

The "ten thousand things" refer to ordinary reality and cultural forms. Multicultural elders are free of cultural restraints. The ancient Confucian sages respected good manners and proper form, but Taoist elders are different. They treat good manners as straw dogs, that is, empty forms. As an elder, you are free to move from deep inside yourself. You don't burn yourself out on meaningless words or customs that are "empty and yet inexhaustible."

Rather than forcing things, wait until the wind blows, and then follow it. In this way, you are breathed like a "bellows" and do not have to breathe; you are following a cosmic breath.

Following the wind distinguishes worldwork from rigid forms of negotiation procedures, social activism, politics and organizational development. It is different from dispute-resolution, with its arbitration, conciliation, participation, mini-trials and mediators. Process work may use these methods, but it sees winning and resolution as cultural forms.

Remember the episode in Moscow described in Chapter Five when delegates from the Caucasus went to the center of the circle to discuss their conflicts? The accepted decorum for political gatherings — sitting still, listening politely while others speak, waiting your turn — was broken up when we suggested making roles out of the dictator, terrorist and facilitators. A game developed that allowed new insights to arise. The metaskills of water and wind allowed us to both respect and relativize the importance of social communication rituals, many of which deter conflict and inhibit its resolution.

Wind and water do not win. They move, flow, relate. They shift benevolently around communication boundaries towards community. As a worldwork elder, you are interested in sustainable culture based upon nature. This means being more than polite, politically correct or neutral.

No Mind 49

The Tao Te Ching describes what I call "no mind" in Chapter 49.

No Mind

The Sage has no set mind;
He takes the mind of others as his mind.

The good, I am good to them.
The not-good, I am also good to them.
This is the goodness of nature.
The trustworthy, I trust them.
The not-trustworthy, I also trust them.
This is the trust of nature.[6]

The no-mind metaskill is about accepting rather than evalu-ating people, seeing things through their eyes. The most widely-held public vision is that everyone should be "good," that is, display no conflict, get along, adapt and, above all, not deviate from socially accepted norms. This vision gives rise to a cultural rigidity that represses diversity and human nature. Divisions into good and bad force us to hide parts of ourselves. Culture rewards the good guys, and puts the bad guys either in jail or in psychiat-ric hospitals, or simply tries to ignore them.

But the "good" and the "not good" are both desperately needed. Together they can be trusted to bring about the process that seeks to manifest. Neither sunshine nor stormy weather is good or bad. When it rains, we don't get angry at storms. That would be futile; storms will always be with us.

The elder knows that the terms "good" and "bad" are only relative to a given community; what people call "bad" is simply the timespirit that "the good" are having trouble with. For the elder, "the bad are as good as the good." As an elder, you need more than compassion for people. You need tolerance for nature. Try to accept things when they seem against you. Notice what is actually happening, including the invisible processes. Can you become tolerant of what others might call "bad" processes like fury, jealousy, competition, sexism and racism? Let them surface. Wait and watch. What begins as a terrible conflict then becomes ice turning to water, as a Tibetan Buddhist might say.

If you resist events, they solidify into abusive personal and cultural forms. Even when people seem to be taking over your job, let it be. Learn, lose, be water, be wind. Maybe your time is up. Discover new, better facilitators.

Until now, most leaders, facilitators, therapists and organiza-tional developers have said that world problems are not fun. True, conflict is difficult. There is nothing fun about oppression. But you suffer more if you conflict with conflict. If you are simply present and aware and don't evaluate people, what culture calls conflict becomes spirit.

How can you arrive at this detached position? Doing the opposite. It takes some of us many years of struggling against the river, of pushing and straining, before we accept life.

THE WORK BELONGS TO EVERYONE

Many cultures in the West advance heroic individualism. They reward individual power and individual charisma. We need to learn from community-oriented cultures that reward individuals for their ability to work in groups. While Western groups assign tasks to individuals, many Asian communities, for instance, assume whole groups are responsible for a given task. Their elders are admired, not for long-winded speeches, but for being able to say just the right thing in a few sentences at just the right moment.

Don't usurp the group's attention. That's an abuse of the media power of being heard and seen. If you follow the white Western model, you may occupy too much of the group's time. If you feel self-important, your striving for success can irritate everyone, regardless of how wise your words are. You will remind other people of their oppressors and enslavers. On the other hand, if you are attached to a feeling of inferiority, you remind groups of another of their worst problems: not taking a stand when the moment has come to do so.

Elders know that awareness and detachment ebb and flow. You can't always sustain awareness, or be both inside and outside a conflict at the same time. Few of us can or should manage multicultural conflict alone under fire. Besides, it is more fun to work in a team — especially if the team has first worked out its own relationship problems. We raise people's awareness. We need people to help raise ours.

Teamwork involves spontaneous, organic consensus that sees everyone's view as part of the community. There can be no view that is against community. This type of consensus does not insist on one thing and repress another. It is an agreement to go for the time being in a certain direction and has no further significance. Be open, but don't insist that others be open too. Instead, model how to follow.

CONSENSUS AND SPIRITUALITY

Teamwork depends on the sense of community, and on everyone's interest and consent in what is happening. Consensus has at least three phases: it can be a state, a goal or a kind of awareness. The most common meaning of "consensus" is that particular state *ar*

State

of a group's mind in which everyone agrees about something. Consensus is that special, temporary group condition in which people move unanimously together in a particular direction.

But consensus can also be a goal. Then unanimous agreement becomes not just a momentary state but the prescribed direction, the end result we seek, where we "should be" going. Such a goal *Goal* has both advantages and disadvantages. There is less friction if we can all agree to something. On the other hand, those who do not agree are likely to be marginalized by accusations of disturbing the community. Then making consensus a goal comes into direct opposition with the process of deep democracy.

Finally, consensus can be an aspect of awareness. In this case, *awareness* you as facilitator share your awareness with everyone. You make statements for everyone's agreement or disagreement, such as, "I notice that the group as a whole seems to be moving in this or that direction." Or, "I notice that many are going in this direction, but a few seem to be moving in another. Where shall we move next?" These statements invite other group members to share what they notice.

Worldwork needs more than the state or goal of consensus. It requires teamwork around the process of awareness.

Leaders know how to push for consent. The multicultural elder, however, is spiritual. By focusing on awareness, an elder makes something magical happen. Unexpected solutions appear at the right moment.

As an elder, you see beyond the moment the rest of us are stuck in and remind us of things we have forgotten. You also recognize rank and culture, but realize no one culture or ranking system is absolute. The rest of us participate in the ten thousand things called culture, climbing the ladder of rank and thereby creating the world problems we live in. Or we shoot others down and detest the world.

Climbing up, falling down, stepping on one another, oblivious to our actions — no matter what we are and do, you as an elder see us all as your children. Fate requires some of us to sleep, others must conflict, applying force to change this world of oppression, rank and pain. Thanks to you, we can sometimes laugh as well.

NOTES

1. Amy Mindell, *Metaskills: The Spiritual Art of Therapy.*
2. *The Wisdom of Lao Tse,* edited and with an introduction by Lin Yutang.
3. *Tao Te Ching, The Book of Meaning and Life by Lao Tzu.* Trans. and commentary by Richard Wilhelm. Translated into English by H.G. Ostwald.
4. *The Tao Te Ching,* trans. Ellen Chen.
5. Ellen Chen says, "The non-human way of heaven and earth means the absence of design. To act humanely is to choose this and reject that..."
6. Chen, op. cit.

14

Violence & Equanimity

DEALING WITH VIOLENCE MAY challenge some of your deep-est beliefs. You need to reconsider what these are even to learn the skills necessary to sit in the circle of fire called community.

The metaskill of being like water and following the Tao helps solve almost any conflict, regardless of the issues. Many facilitators accept Taoism in principle, though, and turn against the process in practice. For instance, facilitators everywhere say, at one time or another, that people who are mean and angry are not "good."

KEEPING ANGER FROM PUSHING OUR BUTTONS

Negotiators, politicians, organizational development experts and psychotherapists sometimes moralize by tell-ing people they should get beyond anger. Trying to pre-scribe behavior, they act as if they had spiritual or social rank. They basically say, "Thou shalt transcend fury. Thou shalt not blame or be greedy!"

The truth is, very few people can follow prescriptions for any form of behavior, including, "Don't blame." Other people's anger pushes our buttons. It reminds us of old abuse issues, and instead of working out the problems, we try to stop the people from being angry. We warn them that anger makes them less worthwhile and they will be punished for it.

How do you go about developing the skills and metaskills for processing anger and violence? To begin with, you need to be familiar with these states and not be surprised by them. You gain a greater sense of personal safety and trust by studying fury. If you know these states in yourself and in others, you will be less surprised, afraid or overwhelmed when they show up in extreme circumstances, in personal life or in large groups.

DEALING WITH YOUR FEAR OF ANGER

The following questions may help remind you about the nature of anger and rage. They may be difficult to answer, because past abuse issues are at stake. I am imagining, at this point, that the reader has already done at least some work on these issues.

1. Recall a person or group of people who made you very nervous or afraid because of their anger.

2. Were you surprised or shocked by them? How did they act that was different from what you had imagined would happen?

3. Did you issue moral prescriptions against them or tell them about your abuse issues?

4. Remember what they looked like. How did they behave when they attacked you or others? What did they sound like? How did your body respond to them? How does it respond now as you remember this incident?

5. Imagine or remember what this person's or group's issues might be. What made them so angry or tough? What were their feelings? When were they the objects of abuse or revenge? Were they afraid of something? How were they

vulnerable? How did you see their vulnerability or was it hidden?

Remember that the way people behave in conflict does not represent all that they are, their whole selves. Rage and vengefulness are provoked by the world; they arise with good reason.

Study your answers to the above questions. If you can understand yourself and others, you will be able to deal with violence better.

HIGH AND LOW DREAMS

If you have studied people when they are seething with anger or in shock from someone else's, you may run into another problem — your "high dreams." Amy and I created this term to mean your deepest beliefs and highest hopes, your expectations that people will live up to some ideal — for instance, the notion that people will always be sweet-tempered. High dreams describe the world you want to create. You may have a high dream that people will always be kind to you and will not surprise or hurt you. You may wish people would always be fair and not lose their tempers.

On the one hand, high dreams can keep you engaged in life; on the other, they can be pipe dreams that cut you off from reality. In the first case, they underlie and strengthen your world view; in the second, they make you co-dependent. You may stay with an abusive situation or person because your dreaming makes you believe things will get better. If you are unaware of these dreams, when events thoroughly shake your world, you wake up one morning and despair. Individuals, groups and whole societies have been hurt when high dreams of, say, a classless society were shattered.

When the bubble bursts, you fall into your "low dream." A low dream occurs when you are in shock about the nature of people, groups, or life. You get depressed and sick. You lose hope, walk out, go back to drugs, swear you'll never go near human beings again, or feel like killing yourself.

For example, suppose you have a high dream that the person with whom you are in relationship will understand your needs and give you support. Then, just when you want someone to lean on, your partner has a big deadline at work and does not fulfill your expectation. You fall into your low dream. Whereas you thought you were the first priority in your partner's life, you now "see" yourself as the last. You issue an ultimatum, pack your things, and walk out. This is how most of us act in relationships. When they go well, we are in our high dream of heaven on earth, and everyone loves us. When the high dream crashes, we are bitter and berate ourselves for having been so stupid.

When you facilitate a group whose vision has crashed or whose leader has been a disappointment, remember low dreams. Otherwise you will wonder why the group members are so depressed. Recall one of your high dreams, what the destruction of that dream was like, how it felt to enter your low dream. That will help you feel compassion for others.

When businesses and organizations, cities and nations hire a conflict-resolution practitioner of one sort or another, the field is usually in the grip of a low dream. They will say, "We had great visions and enthusiasm, but now there is no hope. There's too much trouble and too many bad feelings to deal with."

As the facilitator, you can recognize low dreams by such symptoms as violence, apathy and waning group confidence. Many have given up and are walking out. You must find out what their high dream was. Perhaps their greatest spiritual beliefs have been crushed.

I worked once for a large organization that had a world-changing high dream and had been enjoying a lot of success. When it turned out their leaders were embezzling, hundreds of people fell into a low dream. They called themselves a "dysfunctional organization." Their low dream said that now they could trust no one. Many people in the group became physically ill. In their low dream, everything looked impossible, hopeless.

Watch your own high dreams as a facilitator. Do they call for people to change? As I pointed out in the last chapter, an elder assumes that people are exactly what they are meant to be. Perhaps they are full of mundane characteristics like greed, envy, vengefulness and abusiveness. Can you accept them? Better yet, can you change yourself to love them?

Try seeing your own enemies, friends and neighbors as they are in the moment, not as you would like them to be. Although they are your friends today, remember that next week they may be your attackers. Remember that, historically, very few people have managed to uproot from themselves the tyrant, the monarch, the oppressor, the abuser or the one seeking revenge. It's time we learn to expect negativity and to move with it.

Luckily, blasting a high dream to bits does not always result in permanent depression. When we look back, it may seem as if our high dreams had to be exploded in order to prepare the ground for an even more comprehensive view of the world.

Spirituality And Conflict: Sun And Rain

If you work on yourself or trouble in the world, you are slowly led to the conclusion that negativity and aggression are as central to human nature as love. Being good or bad no longer seem to be the problem. You begin to think that the spirit, or whatever you call the origin of life, is more than opposing forces; it is the process of movement between the polarities. Eventually, it erases them.

You no longer think it's a sin to be angry, or that only bad people raise their voices. You understand that everybody is needed to help express what's in the air.

There are many belief systems that see the spirit as a diverse energy with many colors and actions. I am reminded of the spirit Shiva, seen by the people of India as both creator and destroyer. The spirit or energy of nature seems to make trouble and all kinds of havoc, in part to clear the ground for something new.

Holding unconsciously to our high dreams about life may even provoke nature to bring us trouble. Praying only for peace may not work if we do not pray for consciousness of rank, if we want only to pursue that old sense of peace while supporting the old injustices suffered by those at the periphery of power positions. If we are not careful about perpetuating high dreams that look up to peace and down on angry people, nothing has changed.

While others criticize the anger and vehemence around them, you as an elder accept them as part of nature. Remember Bernice Reagon Johnson (Chapter Eleven), who said that, while most people sing about healing waters, she sings about turbulent waters. "Trouble," she stated, "brings us together."

If I were a Zen master, my conflict-resolution koan would be to understand the sentence:

Rain follows sunshine.

LINEAR AND NON-LINEAR COMMUNICATION

The new paradigm in communication begins with the acceptance of tension and chaos. The old viewpoint was in a hurry to resolve conflict into harmony and thought of contestants as staked in clearly marked positions.

From the new viewpoint, dialogue is the goal. There are no permanent roles. Anyone can be in any role. At the same time, the roles themselves are in flux. Even the physical organization of group processes vary. There may be a traditional setting with people sitting on one side or the other of a table. Or everyone, including you, may sit in a circle or in concentric circles. People can begin speaking from any point on the circle, one at a time or many at a time. Some may approach the center and speak from there to one another. Or there may be dialogue between those in the center and those on the periphery.

In the new paradigm, you need to be able to negotiate even when chaos is occurring. Instead of judging the content — right and wrong, guilty and innocent, good and bad — notice what the moment-by-moment process is. Two basic kinds of communication occur in every conflict. One is linear, the other non-linear.

LINEARITY IS COOL

Linear interaction is the "cooler" style. The parties communicate one at a time and stick to the subject. The facilitator can enable the accusations of one party to be addressed before the accusations of the other party come forward. People may be angry, but clarity prevails.

Many cultures and communities — Eastern and Western, cosmopolitan and indigenous — prefer linearity. They send those in conflict from the meeting place, hoping they will change. Western mediators using Eurocentric styles in business and government typically ignore, depreciate or punish emotional people. Psychological institutes and spiritual centers also tend to display intolerance towards them.

Linear communication has the advantage of addressing the content and details of disagreements. People's need to be protected from violence is respected. Both those in the battle and those outside it can understand what is happening. Use the linear style when people who have had long-standing conflict ask to understand one another, and when everyone is ready to make agreements concerning safety and protection.

The disadvantages of linearity are that strong emotions may be repressed by linear styles, and the feelings and style of marginalized groups may be ignored. One person speaks at a time and the voices of others must wait. This is why negotiations between groups at war often fail; peace is made in linear style at the negotiation table between a few people, while the real feelings of the millions of people in the background are ignored. Negotiators would succeed better if they remembered to represent feelings as well as ideas.

NON-LINEARITY HAS MOVEMENT

Mainstream people sometimes fear non-linear communication because they fall into it only when they are furious or depressed. But this communication style has advantages too.

In general, non-linear interactions are characterized by dialogue that circles instead of proceeding in a straight line. It's not only fury or depression that bring on non-linear communication. Sometimes feelings create a relaxed atmosphere in which thought seems to meander, with people sometimes talking at the same time. All you can understand is the overall tone or good feeling.

Non-linear interaction can lead not only to unknown experiences not on the agenda, but to violence as well. This happens sometimes when one party accuses another of something and, without waiting for the first to finish, those accused defend themselves by making the same or another accusation against the attacker. If the first party is not able or does not want to hear the second, the second becomes more vehement and aggressive in order to get its message across. Both parties become increasingly aggressive. Everyone refuses to listen. Emotions, but not issues, are addressed. Anger escalates. Voices are raised in threats and counter-threats until someone walks out or threatens physical violence.

Finally someone wins and someone loses. If a facilitator notices hot spots and edges, however, non-linearity can lead to a real peace. There are many advantages to non-linear communications. When they occur in the area of conflict-resolution, non-linear escalations allow underlying emotions such as vengefulness and fury to find expression. People can express themselves simultaneously without being frustrated by a one-to-one, linear agenda. Non-linearity enables people who have been merely cordial to know each other emotionally. Emotional exchange can be preventative medicine against future violence.

One disadvantage of non-linear escalation is that rational discussion of the issues must wait until after things calm down. In addition, unless facilitators are trained in such communication, there is the danger of violence. People who are unaccustomed to angry confrontations often become fearful and refuse to participate. Non-linear interactions require more psychological ability and experience from facilitators than do linear processes.

How do you determine which communication style to use? You don't. The people, the times, the issue and the country determine that. Your job is to notice the style, explain it to the participants and work with the process.

In Europe and the United States, the linear style is generally used for town meetings and open forums, especially when the public is watching on television. Such town meetings seem to automatically conform to mainstream communication methods. This style gives parties who are furious with one another a chance to hear one another, sometimes for the first time. Remember the meeting described in Chapter Three, where gay and lesbian activists in Oregon met with a fundamentalist group, the Oregon Citizens Alliance? Both sides were able to hear each other for the first time. Many said they were happy to understand the opposing party.

Non-linear escalations seem chaotic to the mainstream, and are definitely more emotional than what the mainstream typically tolerates. When linear communication fails, or when no facilitators are present to catch the edges in the linear conversation and enable it to go deep, non-linearity and escalation follow.

When one party accuses another and the second party counter-accuses, worldwork elders first encourage both parties to deal with the first accusation before dealing with the second. Otherwise, both parties raise their voices to be heard. Then non-linearity occurs. The Oakland conference on racial issues discussed in Chapter Eleven provides an example of a linear style — trying to explain a conflict-resolution procedure — followed by non-linearity, where everyone began speaking at once. Escalation was followed by a real coming together.

EVERY GROUP NEEDS BOTH LINEARITY AND NON-LINEARITY

I remember an incredible conflict between Latinos and whites. We were about three hundred people, debating the issue of migrant workers from Latin America entering California. For hours people spoke politely and respected one another. Everyone wanted to be open to the opinions of others. While linearity prevailed, there was nevertheless a sense of fear in the air. Somehow, the group could not get down to what it really felt about the issues.

Latino workers spoke of a glass ceiling that kept migrant farm help out of work. At one point, a Latina complained that she was not able to express herself completely and felt upset by a white woman. That ended the linear discussion. Suddenly, a Latino man came forward and started yelling about how much agony he'd had to go through and had never expressed. For years, he was forced to be nice in order to survive. He begged for understanding, but no one could give it to him just yet. Before he even finished, a lesbian woman stood up and said she could wait no longer, her trouble was agonizing. She too had been marginalized. It seemed that the emotional freedom claimed by the Latinos now allowed all kinds of emotions to come forth.

The meeting entered a non-linear phase with many things happening at once. Whites said they wanted to be understood and loved as individuals, not as white, but as people without reference to color. The Latinos complained again that whites never thought of anyone but themselves. The escalations and chaos increased, and dozens of people began to debate privately in the midst of this immense group. There was still a certain amount of focus on the very center of the group, where a heated, linear debate was occurring between the original Latina and a white woman. Each insisted on being accepted by the other. Our facilitation team helped them go over their edges until they did begin to accept one another.

The atmosphere started to change. It was beginning to look more like a fiesta than a conflict. Someone yelled in truly linear style, "Time for lunch." The entire scene came to a fast and good-humored end. After lunch, everyone seemed content to settle down in smaller groups and work out solutions to the ethnic conflicts and specific issues at hand in a linear fashion. Later the white owner of a large company told me that he had never understood Latinos before. Now he loved them! He promised to change his company accordingly.

Understanding linearity and non-linearity allows you to work with intense situations. Yet the spirit of change can never be entirely understood. It is swift, unpredictable and amazing.

War And The Dojo

Where do you get the training necessary to develop spiritual metaskills for this work? You need a *dojo*. Dojo is the Japanese word for the room where martial artists train with one another. You can learn non-linearity in large groups, but your own relationships are the best dojos I know. If you can handle the flow between linear and non-linear communication in your personal life, you will be well prepared as a facilitator.

When you experience friction, watch the movement of the spirit. Practice conflict. Get into it when it is not yet serious. Notice when you are using a linear and when a non-linear style of communication. Try consciously switching back and forth instead of just sliding from one to the other. See if you can work with double signals, that is, intentional messages and hidden messages. Watch for edges and hot spots.

Conflict and war alter us; we become strangers to ourselves sometimes, as low and high dreams emerge unexpectedly. While most people fear that conflict will change them into either victims or deranged aggressors, you, the elder, should welcome the opportunity to get to know yourself in conflict. Perhaps the following questions will help.

1. With whom have you had a recent conflict?

2. How did you behave?

3. What were your typical double signals? That is, which experiences were you afraid to express directly? Which did you refuse to admit even to yourself?

4. How were your double signals connected to your rank and vengefulness?

5. What do you like best and least about yourself in relationship? Get to know the part you like least. Try speaking to it and keeping an open mind. Think about it, what it wants, how it feels. Try to find out more about it by imagining or acting it out.

6. What was linear or non-linear about the relationship process? Which style is more natural to you? If you used only one, would the other have been useful?

Ask your partner to help you analyze the dynamics of what happens between you. What emotional states do the two of you go through in conflict? Worldwork studies cannot be done alone. Seek out the people you are closest to as your teachers in this work.

ONE-SIDEDNESS REPRESSES THE SPIRIT

If your friends tell you that you behave one way but you feel another way, you probably repress a part of yourself. This also keeps a timespirit down, and provokes others. For example, if you act kind and disavow your own vehemence, people may attack you vehemently in compensation. Or, if you claim to be open but secretly feel that you want to moralize and criticize others for their behavior, you may be confused when people become defensive around you. It's better to know yourself and state your views directly. That leads to open debate.

The point is not that you are whole and balanced, but that you are able to notice your own one-sidedness and use it in process. Watch your dreams for parts of yourself you have forgotten. Then you can enter with others into a process of change.

While I was a student in Switzerland, I was walking down the street in Zurich with one of my teachers when we were approached by another student who began criticizing the teacher for being too disciplined during an exam. The teacher did not defend himself; instead he burst out laughing and told the student a dream. The previous night, he had dreamed that he had not been strict enough with the students. The dream was right; he was always too good-hearted.

The other student wasn't the least bit satisfied, but before he could speak, the teacher apologized for acting more tolerant than he was towards the student. "I was a fake because I am not un ?

completely aware of the disciplinarian part of myself. Sorry, but be happy," he said. "Next time I'll flunk you if you don't do better!"

We were all surprised and laughed at his sudden ability to be tough. That ended the discussion. The student knew where he stood and prepared thoroughly for final exams.

My teacher knew himself well. He had a lot of psychological rank and used it for everyone's benefit. Best of all, he showed me how to follow nature and let things move from one opposite to the other in the dojo of relationships. In this interaction, both my teacher and the other student represented the spirits of the moment, kindness and discipline.

DETACHMENT: THE RESULT OF BEING SHOT AT

Relationships and public work put you in the line of fire; these dojos are places of extreme tension, and death and rebirth as well. After you have been attacked and shot at enough, you seem to get a few holes in you. Then things go through you better, and your identity gets lighter. You become naturally more neutral and detached.

More complete detachment in worldwork comes from burning your wood. Once you burn through your rage, you need not worry about staying cool in conflict; you are naturally more detached. When being shot at leaves you somewhat detached from your identity, you begin to admire, or at least respect, the courage you see in the most impossible person and your most belligerent opponent.

GOING OVER DOUBLE EDGES

Most organizations are not aware of their one-sidedness and how it causes chaos and divides the community into parts. Businesses are not aware of how they abuse their workers; cultures are not aware of how those who do not go along with the mainstream are marginalized. You get stuck in relationships, and the world gets stuck with itself — the spirit cannot flow — because those in conflict arrive at edges. There are at least two edges in a communication system. These are what I call "double edges." The double edge is the key, in blocked crisis, to letting the water flow again.

Think of a relationship between a man and a woman. If she goes over her edge, yells and expresses all of her needs, but he sits around and gets insulted without saying so, she will feel relieved for the present, but he will hold a grudge. The system has two edges; both must be crossed for the water to flow freely again. She has gone over hers, but he has not been able to go over his.

In groups, the same things happen. If two subgroups are in conflict and one goes over the edge and the other does not, then the facilitator will be accused by the second group of favoring the first group. The second group is insulted and plots revenge.

This often happens when a group that has been peripheral to the mainstream speaks out. In public meetings in the United States, Native Americans, Latinos, Asians or African Americans may go over their edge and speak about the pain of racism. If whites do not respond with anything more than, "I am sorry, I feel guilty," there may soon be a backlash.

BACKLASH

The mainstream acts politically correct in the foreground but revolts and exerts its power insidiously in the background. If all parties do not go over the edge, no one is served. In the background, the mainstream privately accuses the world of favoring the "agenda of racism."

Backlash is not inevitable, but is due to the facilitators' missing a double edge. We should have warned everyone, after people who felt oppressed spoke, that if the people accused of oppression did not respond by sharing their feelings, there would be backlash later on.

It's important to get not just one party to speak about its experiences, but everyone. To get over the double edge, you must help the mainstream to be "politically incorrect." They must admit they want the status quo to endure and that they are upset at having their tranquillity disturbed. Unless they clearly say, "Those troublemakers, why are they always complaining?" no true understanding can occur. The same is true in business. If middle management speaks out against upper management, backlash could mean that the people with less rank get fired. As an elder, you must remember the double edge.

Everyone needs to be free. A community comes together only when the voices that have been kept down can speak and the ones keeping them down can also speak and air their convictions. Otherwise the oppressed claim to be oppressed and so do those in the mainstream. It seems strange, but those in power then think that they must revolt for freedom. When those in power clearly share their views, terrorist tactics among the oppressed are asked to change. In this manner, everyone becomes aware of power and former enemies can become allies.

Working at the double edge is preventative medicine; it might cure a problem before it becomes one. It takes courage to guide people over edges. You need to practice in the dojo, know yourself, remember non-linearity and hot spots. That's where the edges are. But if all the parts of an organization or city are allowed to express themselves and empowered to get over their edges, conflicts dissolve and violence becomes unnecessary. In that moment, everyone realizes that rain and sun follow one another. The whole community seems enlightened. The river again flows.

BELIEF IN THE CIRCLE OF FIRE

A spiritual attitude makes it easier to tolerate anger and move through the double edges to reach understanding and even enlightenment about the nature of the world. The problem is knowing how to develop this attitude, which is so helpful in the unfolding of human processes. To reach transcendence, many religions and spiritual traditions suggest discipline. Various forms of Buddhism and Hinduism, for example, recommend sitting still in the lotus position, even when the knees ache. These traditions teach that if you focus on the pain, it eventually eases.

To maintain such discipline in the face of pain, a person must believe in the presence of great powers or forces. The spiritual practitioner feels that the very act of sitting through painful moments is — paradoxically — the basis for alleviating pain.

The oldest text on yoga from India's legendary spiritual historian, Pantajali, suggests what happens next: "Yoga teaches yoga." This means if you begin with a little discipline, this discipline automatically teaches you awareness and concentration, which increases your original discipline. For purposes of world-work, discipline gives you awareness and finally teaches you how to deal with violence. Discipline and awareness teach you about yourself and about the linear and non-linear communication of others.

How can you find the belief in process that will enable you to sit in the fire of community? I do not have a final answer to this immense question. Perhaps sitting as an elder is a kind of "calling," that is, an inner sense that maintaining equanimity in the midst of adversity will help everyone.

15

The Technique & Tao Of War

WAR IS PART OF THE FLOW of world history. Until now, war has meant a form of devastation that changed the world balance of power, murdering millions. The threat of conventional war is the most complex process for a facilitator to handle; that's why so little is known about it. The potential violence terrifies everyone and makes us want to skirt the issues. But waiting is not the solution.

In addition to nations, families and groups of all sizes go to war, some of them frequently. Small-scale conflicts have a positive side; they enable us to practice becoming warriors in the best sense.

The first step for the facilitator is to notice war. In worldwork, we view war as foremostly a state of consciousness. It has at least five characteristics:

1. *The opponents feel despair.* All those involved feel they have tried everything. They have given up hope that problems can be resolved. They are finished with repressing their instincts in order to avoid hostilities.

2. *The opponents are enemies.* They have decided to treat each other as enemies. They have nothing good to say about each other. People talk like enemies, act like enemies, are enemies.

3. *Each opponent seeks more power.* Each side feels threatened because of some handicap. They don't have as much psychological, social and physical power as the opponent. They don't have enough love, respect, land or money. They insist that the other side is responsible for their deprivation. They walk out of negotiations, issue ultimatums and grow stronger at their opponents' expense. Each side feels things are weighted against it and seeks more power to overcome the opponent.

4. *There is nothing more to learn.* Combatants have abandoned the hope of mutual learning through friendship. Each party rejects any suggestion that they are projecting aspects of themselves onto the other side. They feel the "evil other" is only outside and not inside as well. The atmosphere is electrified with the approaching conflict.

5. *Violence is at hand.* Communication becomes turbulent, then chaotic, then furious. It's the ultimate hot spot. Everybody talks at once, and since nobody listens, feelings escalate. Both sides implicitly plot, then explicitly state that the time has come to replace threats with action. Violence is the chosen alternative to friendship. The time has come to leave the barricades of safety. Everyone is willing to risk losing personal history and life.

WAR BECOMES A SACRED EVENT

Most conflict managers wash their hands of war. But you as an elder will have compassion for the people involved. They are doing the best they can under the circumstances. You know this, because you too have gone through times of war.

Chapter 49 of the ancient Taoist text, *I Ching* or *Book of Changes*, is called "Revolution." It provides a grand prospective:

> It is said, "Times change, and with them their demands. Thus the seasons change in the course of the year. In the world cycle also there are spring and autumn in the life of peoples and nations, and these call for social transformations."[1]

In war, transformation ceases at first; everyone freezes in their respective positions. Severe conflict is dry ice. The hatred of disagreement is so great that the people involved are cold to the point of freezing. But remember, ice is just frozen water and can be melted. You begin melting the ice by focusing on it. You might say, "This is the time of cold that is so deep it almost burns. War is present. Battle is here, that devastating agreement to disagree. People might be hurt. "

Speaking clearly in moments when everyone else is locked in hatred has amazing effects; it places awareness in the foreground. It can soften rage. People remember that there is more to life than war. Tell the opponents how you see them manifesting the five characteristics of war. Do this with impartiality. Say that you believe all those involved are doing their best for both themselves and others.

When you use awareness as a framework, someone else will eventually join you. In this way, you can change a potential brawl into a sacred event. In deep democracy, war, too, can be part of the mysterious Tao.

A NONVIOLENT WAR EXERCISE

Facilitators must be careful not to look down on people and communities in conflict. We have all experienced the state of war at one time or another. We battled with parents, teachers, bosses, spouses, ex-spouses, children, neighbors, political opponents, civil authorities or religious leaders. War is more commonplace than we might like to admit.

We perpetuate war by not understanding it from within, no matter how intensely we experience it. The questions below can help melt the ice when combatants are on the verge of battle. They can also be used at any time as an exercise that will give you insight into your own war-behaviors.

The following nonviolent war exercise is a ritual that transforms mundane hatred and war into a state of awareness that is sacred and spiritual. As such, war is not something that we should try to overcome. It helps us see the events at hand as wild but meaningful. The spiritual warrior respects the events at hand as the gateway to the unknown. We can understand the unknown only by entering into it completely.

1. *Recall a moment of war*. Think of a severe conflict in an intimate or business relationship. Recall the moment when you felt war was necessary, when you gave up on growing with the other person and saw only your enemy. In what ways had your view of the person changed? What had you said about the person when you first met? What were you saying at the moment of war?

2. *Recall your violent moods* when you were in that person's presence or thinking or talking about them. What did you want to do to that person? What did you hope would happen to that person?

3. *Play war*. Using a linear style of communication, talk to an actual enemy, or ask a friend to play that role and practice admitting that you see your enemy as entirely bad. Experiment with admitting that objectivity and negotiation are no longer possible. There has been so much pain that you can't help yourself. All you can do is protect your feelings or lash out.

Now comes the scary part of the exercise. Hold on to your center, your awareness, and at the same time, don't repress your worst feelings. Remember, everything can change when you enter into the process. Consider saying that you are wondering how to destroy your enemy by forcing them to change. Pause and listen to them say the same sorts of things to you.

4. *Switch to a non-linear style*. Remain aware of what goes on inside you. Feel yourself. Set a limit on the time you give yourself and your opponent for the fierce state. Perhaps five minutes. Agree that there will be no physical harm done.

Identify the moment when you decide to attack, and go for it! Allow yourself to be intense, fierce and vehement in your expressions. Let accusations pour out of you, while remaining centered.

You may have no trouble entering into the flow. Or you may experience resistance. You may be ambivalent. Who wants to hurt anyone? Normally, no one wants to put someone else down forcibly. Now all sorts of prejudices you have against your opponent personally and the groups to which your opponent belongs may come to the surface. Don't try to be correct.

Experiment with intensity, but meditate while in battle. Go to war as you go to knowledge — as an intense learning experience. Follow yourself as your fierce feelings unravel. Stay fully aware; watch your own behavior and your opponent's. Listen for voice changes. Notice your posture shift and express it in words like, "I am furious, but I feel myself backing down because I don't want to hurt you." "I am depressed and slumped; my rage has been silenced." Or "I could strike you down!"

Take care that both you and the other warrior do not lose awareness. Follow the signals of change when they come, and return to your ordinary selves. Stay in touch with yourself and the other. Above all, follow and do not lead the trouble. Don't attempt to suppress it. That will only make the trouble worse.

All this is easier to write about than to do. I remember one of the first times I went into battle consciously. What a difficult scene! I was working in a clinic with people who were near death. Many people suffered intensely from their illnesses. One remarkable man, who was dying of AIDS, told us all he had changed dramatically because of his agony. His mind was no longer the same. He was belligerent all the time. He was taking medication against mania, against psychosis, but it did not help. He talked and talked, lashed out at others, made fun of them and could not stop hurting those around him.

I did what I could to quiet him and protect others. I waited and was as tolerant as possible, knowing about the intense suffering AIDS can cause. Doctors who were present were begging me to let them give him more medication against his mania. I told him I could understand his anger; he had been hurt in the past and was suffering so much now. I tried to understand, until I could no longer hold myself back. Instead of taking the doctors' offer to bring him down with medication, I pulled myself together and said: "Your time has come. You won't stop talking, and it's time for war. I feel nothing else can help. We cannot go on together. In my opinion, you must change."

He went on raving about how stupid everyone was and insisted that I too was a moron. Finally, I let go. "Shut up and sit down. You are hurting everyone and wasting the last moments of everyone's life. You are a blithering idiot and I can't stand you. SHUT UP!"

I used all my rank against my better judgment. I was a therapist; he was a client. What a moment. I was almost devastated with the sadness of the overall situation. I hated him for forcing me to lose my temper, and I detested myself for doing so.

He paused for a moment. Then he went on. "You are a wimp, you wimp. You are chicken!"

"If you don't sit down, I will sit you down," I said. "I am ready to fight. Watch out!" I knew that I wouldn't harm him, but I was now almost beside myself. Suddenly I saw his head go down. I remembered the *I Ching* and thought to myself, "Aha, the seasons are changing." I said, "You are hurt, and I have done it because I was too dumb to know what else to do."

He fell silent, and so did I. We sat like that for some time. Then I risked moving an inch closer to him, and he moved toward me and we embraced. I had hated him, but I also loved him dearly. I told him so.

The group broke up for the day. The next day I went up to him to apologize, but he assured me I should not feel bad. I had saved his life, he said. "I was going to kill myself because I felt that this manic state of mind proved I was a failure. If I had been forced to take more of that medication, I would have killed myself."

Each time you go into awesome, war-like interactions, it seems like the first time. Yet, psychologically, something changes in you. You are sad you had to get into all that, yet it was better to get in than stay out. You are humbled because you realize that somehow destiny was at the controls.

FEAR AND STALEMATES: THE FACILITATOR'S ALLIES

When you facilitate war and people lose their tempers, look closely for expressions that indicate fear of being hurt. Notice signs of withdrawal. That too stems from fear.

Fear is important. Opponents who are furious get attached to acting powerfully; they repress their fear. When fear becomes evident, it can protect and make change happen. De-escalation occurs. Things become safer.

If combatants become afraid of continuing, they may need to express their fear of being hurt. This could be a signal to discontinue the non-linear style and its escalation. If you encourage a switch to a linear style, they may find relief and a sense of safety in answering each accusation with a defense.

Watch for symmetrical accusations. In violent arguments, people often accuse each other of the same thing.

Someone says, "You are evil."

The other responds, "You are worse."

The first says, "No one is worse than you!"

Listen for ultimatums: "If you don't change, I will x, y and z." Call an ultimatum by its name; it raises everyone's awareness. Ultimatums are desperate attempts to break through stalemates. Sometimes you can help by saying to the person who has issued an ultimatum, "I hear you. I am listening." Or, "How courageous and strong you seem."

Stalemates are dangerous. Sometimes they happen because no one noticed the stalemate. Keep your ears open and say, for example, "Stalemate. The time of being blocked is here. No one knows what to do, other than walk out. We are stuck for the moment."

Such awareness helps everyone change and move on. One party eventually admits to an accusation and breaks the deadlock. Or something emotional happens, as in the battle with the man with AIDS, which makes everyone drop the issue and focus on feelings that have never been expressed.

Everything in the battle, including stalemate, is part of the river called community. Don't work against a stalemate by trying to force things to happen.

Remember the two women's conflict in which we stopped in the midst of battle at a point of stalemate? One went home and dreamed about a yogi. Solutions arrive in many ways.

THE TAO OF BREAKING UP AND COMING TOGETHER

Severe conflict can threaten to separate or be facilitated to bring a community together. Sometimes it seems as if a couple or family war becomes the central spirit for a whole organization. Can you think of relationship problems, battles, feuds, or conflicts between groups or organizations which became central to the community or the whole world? Think about how ethnic conflicts in another part of the world become central to your country.

The trials that monopolized U.S. media in the early 1990s, such as the Menendez trial, the Clarence Thomas vs. Anita Hill hearings, the Lorena and John Bobbit trial and the O.J. Simpson trial, illustrate a country's using a couple or individual to work out national issues about racism and sexism. The combatants are forced to be central timespirits for the world around them.

What seems like a personal battle can turn into the whole field for organizations. When this happens, privacy becomes impossible. You have to go into, rather than avoid, the issues at hand. I recommend to large organizations that they form a framework or a container in which a central conflict involving a few people can be facilitated. Others look on while the battle evolves. Conflicting parties can then be seen clearly as roles in the organization.

Sometimes the large group seems unable to concentrate. It keeps interrupting the combatants. Suppose a man and a woman are in the center, conflicting around their personal and leadership issues. The whole organization has been gossiping about them. Now they are battling it out. But the group continuously interrupts; everyone seems to know best. The combatants may have reached an edge, and the group may be trying to push them through their communication block. Or people may have been so repressed that their need to express themselves emotionally makes them unwilling to watch a couple working out their conflicts.

In this situation, you as an elder might notice whether the group shows a tendency to inhibit those in the center. Ask others to enter the center and take sides as well. Watch for edges and hot spots, and help people remain awake.

If the onlookers begin to discuss things with one another and still cannot concentrate on the center, you can also take this as part of the flow of group process. Ask the group for consensus to break up into smaller groups, each trying to process or resolve the conflicts at hand.

Breaking into smaller groups enables people to experience how the problems discussed in the center are actually their own problems. Breaking into smaller groups happens automatically during pauses in group work, which is why resolutions sometimes appear after a recess.

If one particular subgroup wants the complete attention of the large group, then it may choose to come to the center. Don't favor either separation or staying together. They are simply two polarities in the life of a community. There is a time for coming together and a time to break up when the large group becomes blocked, has gotten to an edge, has run out of time or cannot go further. Perhaps participants need to think things over for themselves. They want to reflect on whether the group battle does or does not reflect their interior conflict. People may also start breaking up because things are settled. Follow the natural flow of coming together and breaking up. Follow the Tao of war, chaos and peace.

THE SAMURAI AND THE RAIN

Amy and I were first invited to help Esalen in the 1980s. We reported on that organization in some detail in our book *Riding the Horse Backwards*. At the time, Esalen was one of the premier psychological growth communities in the United States. It had launched Fritz Perls, Gestalt psychology, Rolfing and many other people and techniques in the humanistic psychology movement. After its spiritual leader, Dick Price, died, the Esalen community took a precipitous path. It was on the verge of disintegrating because of management and staff conflicts.

We arranged an all-community meeting as the quickest way to solve problems and stop the loss of time and creativity through gossip about conflicts. When the community came together the first night, people were terrified of the anger that had built up because of unresolved disputes. As people began to speak, it started to rain. This was noteworthy because northern California had suffered from drought for years.

Esalen became a spiritual warrior and went to battle as it went into everything else, seeking situations from which it could grow. As the timespirits of the management and the staff went over edges and raged, it seemed as if an entire race of wrathful demons had been let loose. It was as close to war as a group can come without actually injuring anyone.

The process ended in two hours. The subsections of the group continued to work for several days. It rained and rained. The community found its center again. Esalen recreated itself, almost from scratch. And it rained and rained. It was as if a blocked process had been preventing the flow of seasons from summer into fall.

I remember another such dramatic event in Japan during the summer of 1994, when the country was suffering a terrible drought. In certain areas, no one was allowed to use water for 16 hours a day.

The group we worked with was focusing on changes that needed to be made in Japanese culture. The subject of Japanese men putting down Japanese women came up during one of the first evenings. A man told a story about how women much older than he and in the same position had to serve him in his job at an insurance company. Everyone seemed shocked, but no one knew what to do to change that situation.

I asked what had happened to the culture of the Samurai, the spiritual warriors who fought for communities. Some Japanese men said their heroic instincts died with the end of the Second World War. Today the Samurai could only be found sublimated in business.

Some women stated that they would settle the problem if the men did not. After they spoke, silence reigned again. A large, powerful man got up to play the role of the Patriarch who gladly kept women down. He said, "Down with them" and again silence reigned.

Then the Samurai came back to life! Suddenly, as if out of the clear blue sky, a remarkable, small man arose and, shrieking in the most terrifying way, bolted like lightening across the room. In one leap he landed right in front of the Patriarch. As the two men stood face to face, the Samurai seemed half the size of the Patriarch. The Patriarch laughed and assured the Samurai that he was not intimidated.

The Samurai made such violent, war-like movements that even I was afraid he might hurt someone. But the Patriarch did not move. The Samurai, centered in himself, used his full awareness and, looking the Patriarch straight in the eye, said with great intent, "You, dear opponent, are terrified of me. I know because your legs are shaking."

Everyone cheered, and the Patriarch agreed. He said he would be happy to change.

A spiritual warrior was needed to enter into conflict, make war and fight for culture and change. Everyone got the message. It pays to be centered if you are going to be vehement. Better yet, the rain began. It poured and poured. The waters flowed again and filled the dry reservoirs. It rained so much the water flooded the train tracks and the roads. Amy and I almost missed our flight back to the States.

That Samurai was amazing. He modeled how to stand up against authorities. The entire community was a spiritual warrior. It entered into what seemed to be an impossible war. It sat in the fire and helped turn ice to water.

THE RIVER OF COMMUNITY

Once a community gets together in an open forum and deals with its most difficult issues, it knows itself from a new angle. The atmosphere improves. The community proceeds to work on action plans, business goals, contracts and social issues.

Just as important, however, the community has experimented and discovered that, if violence is admitted and addressed, it is less destructive than if it is repressed.

Going consciously into battle is an intense experience, but one that revitalizes everyone. You are renewed in hope. You find not only solutions to issues, but something more precious. You find that a battle does not mean the end of the world, but the beginning of the river called community.

NOTE

1. Wilhelm/Baynes, *The I Ching*, p. 190.

16

The Awareness Revolution

WORLDWORK AFFECTS YOU as a citizen of a city, a state and the world. Eldership helps liberate the river of community so it can flow again.

As you become an elder, you change inside. With rank consciousness, your personal relationships become deeper. Your group and city are glad to see you coming. Issues and problems are not only to be solved; they are paths to community. Your community realizes that the way it deals with conflict determines history.

By growing into eldership, you and your group make a revolution in human consciousness.

REVOLUTION: MORE RADICAL THAN REFORM

Reform alters certain aspects of a society but does not aim, as revolution does, at the replacement of existing social, economic or political structures. Reform is incremental. It proceeds in a linear, step-by-step fashion.[1] For example, the Civil Rights Movement in the United States during the 1960s was a reform movement. It attacked aspects of capitalism and democracy, but did not destroy them. It did not change the central, existing institutions. It tried, step-by-step, to open them up to full participation by minorities.

If things don't change enough with reform, revolution follows. This is the lesson of history. From the viewpoint of process work, revolution occurs when the governing powers are unaware of rank and of the resulting oppression and they ignore hot spots. Revenge and terrorism follow. Polarities become rigid. The system reaches an edge. Its identity is endangered. It is unable to recognize those who are marginalized — those on the other side of the edge — and forces them into increasingly peripheral, distant and untenable positions. After trying and failing to obtain a transformation of the existing leadership, the marginalized group is left with the choice of overthrowing the authorities or submitting and dying internally.

Discontent is replaced by apathy, then despair, anger, and finally violence and war.

THE FAILURES OF REVOLUTIONS

Revolution is a far more radical process than reform. Revolution suddenly and completely overturns the established political, economic and social structures. Change happens everywhere at the same time. For example, the communist-led Chinese revolution transformed China's entire economy, taking it from the hands of individuals and handing it over to the state. Revolutions in recent times have overthrown regimes in Nicaragua, Vietnam and Cambodia. Unlike reforms, revolutions are not gentle. They come about through violence between insurgents and counter-insurgents.

Through revolution, important aspects of the world have changed. For example, we have more democracy as a legal institution around the world than ever before. Yet, we must not get drunk on our high dreams. Issues and problems have changed, but the manner in which we get along has not. From the viewpoint of process work, revolution of social structures has not changed the individual or our consciousness of relationship. Where awareness and consciousness are concerned, revolutions have in fact been only reforms. They were directed at change of social policy and had too little effect on sustainable community process. As a result, new prescriptions for how people should behave and causal solutions to impending issues took precedence over consciousness — noticing events and following them.

DEMOCRACY: THE ROAD OF BLOOD

A little political theory explains why revolution in our awareness has not occurred. Remember, the word *democracy* comes from the Greek *demokratia*, which means "citizen power." In democracy today, power is shared more than in monarchies, but we should not fool ourselves. The majority has more or less the same power as the old ruler. Democracies are not citizen power; they are majority or mainstream power. This may be why democracies are no more peaceful than the dictatorial systems they supplanted. According to Small, Melvin and Singer, in *The War-Proneness of Democratic Regimes*, 1816-1965, democracies go to war just as often as other systems.

We are still in the age of dictatorship. The road to democracy has been covered with everyone's blood and we continue to travel this road today. Consider the French Revolution. In 1791, French patriots spoke of liberty and reason; they destroyed those ideals in 1792 by enforcing them with the guillotine. Although the revolutionaries toppled the monarchy and tried to create religious freedom, they did so by brutally crushing their opponents, including the Catholic Church. They insisted upon universal suffrage, but for men, not women, and not the indigenous peoples of French colonies. It remained social policy to take Africans as slaves. Revolutions for democracy bring about incremental social change for some, not complete liberation for everyone.

Fighting in the revolution, Napoleon became a brigadier general. Attempts at revolt made him, first, head of the army and, later, first consul with supreme power. In 1804, he declared himself emperor. In the name of freedom and liberty for all, France crushed its enemies, conquering the European continent from the Atlantic to Russia, from the Adriatic to the North Sea. Napoleon freed the serfs and put down monarchs, but was shocked when countries enjoying their new freedom saw him as a dictator, decided to determine their own fates and rebelled against him.

The English philosophers Hume and Locke tried to awaken people to freedom, but they were more popular in France and the new colonies than in England. The American Declaration of

Independence was followed by the French Declaration of the Rights of Man and the Citizen in 1789 and the Constitution of the United States in 1789. All were based on the idea of inalienable, universal and absolute rights — for some, but not everybody.

More recent revolutions in Algeria, China, Russia, Mexico, Vietnam, Cuba, Bolivia, Angola, Mozambique and elsewhere have shown that inalienable rights are far from being universally agreed upon. The agrarian cultures led by peasants, together with an educated elite, interrupted military domination. Although governments and administrations were dissolved, the power problems remained the same, merely better hidden. Visible dictatorship and monarchy disappeared, but oppression remained.

WHAT WE MUST CHANGE

Today we worry about nuclear waste and supplies of fossil fuels. The issues are different, but human nature has not changed. We still have prejudice, egotism, greed and power-hunger. Neither social revolution nor the reform process of ordinary democracy, with its solutions directed at discrete causes, can work with these problems. Awareness is necessary.

In fact, most reforms and revolutions drive problems underground. The globalization of economies and the forcing of nation-state boundaries on diverse ethnic groups who do not choose to be together assure continued trouble. If we take into account as well the vengefulness building in millions of people from racially and economically disadvantaged countries and groups, it's easy to make the prediction that there will be at least as much war in the next century as in the past — unless something changes.

We need changes, not only around specific political and environmental issues, but in our awareness of how we get along together. Worldwork facilitators must have a global picture of things to understand that a radical revolution is at hand with every group process.

All this may have been easier in small tribal settings. In a large multicultural arena, there are no agreed-on rituals, and bombs are waiting to go off. Living only in their own mainstream communities blinds many people to national and international rank. Others who are not part of mainstream communities suffer, get angry and mean, react to abuse, request change, try to reform things, revolt and inevitably take over. Nothing less than a revolution in consciousness, in moment-to-moment awareness, will suffice to change the way we get along together. First we have to change our attitude toward change, open up to trouble and notice how power is used.

The big job for the next century is to deal with the hell we create in spite of our greatest visions and our revolutions. What does it all mean to you? Everything you do influences the world. You can't help being part of the field, even if you are a hermit. So use your awareness. Make a better world.

Ten Concrete Steps To Change The World

If even a few of us go through the following steps now and then, the world will be less like hell and more like home.

1. Ask: "Who wants liberty?" Clarify your basic intent. Keep it in the foreground. The rest will come more easily. Do you want liberty for your whole person or only part of it? Do you want the same for some people and not others? Think of your enemies and people you don't like. Do you want liberty for them? Tell the truth. That's how to begin.

2. Notice and accept where we are. Observe yourself and everyone else. What do people say? How does this differ from what they do? Value both, starting with what we say and do. Then notice all the secondary, unconscious events in groups. Follow these events. Let the group become the leader.

3. Watch for hidden rank and double signals. Remember that those with rank keep it hidden, not necessarily because they are malicious, but because they are blind to it. Even these "bad guys" need understanding. If you have trouble being kind to "bad guys," ask yourself how consciously you use whatever rank you have. Or become a social activist and support others in facilitating. All parts are needed; no one is better than another.

4. Remember the dynamics of revenge. Rank causes revenge. Don't be naive; expect terrorists. Some call them evil, but those who think of themselves as innocent of terrorism are not necessarily any better. They may be the ones with hidden rank.

5. Find your voice and spirit. Many who have been traumatized are too terrified to speak out. There can be no democracy without noticing them. They must be encouraged to do abuse work. And there's no better place to start than with yourself. You are not making an awareness revolution if you get stuck in the roles of the silent one, the terrorist or the leader. You are not making an awareness revolution if you get stuck in any role.

6. Know history and its issues. There are recurring basic motifs regardless of group or nation: love, self-esteem, who's got the money, who's best. No one has ever disposed of these motifs. If you insist on resolving them once and for all, you become a hierarchical antagonist of the human species. The goal of worldwork isn't to create a conflict-free world. After all, some problems may persist to create community. The goal is to follow individuals, groups, nature and the Tao. Follow your God.

7. Develop skills. You must know how to recognize an edge, and don't forget double edges. Notice hot spots, roles and timespirits. Pay attention to the ghosts, the hidden roles no one wants to admit. Think about linear and non-linear communication, reform and revolution, and remain awake to yourself and others during emotional battles.

8. Develop metaskills. Unless you can rise to a meta-level in order to stay clear, unless you possess metaskills, your ordinary skills won't work. No one will trust you. Remember the magic of eldership — it's as simple as that. Connect your highest beliefs to the significance of tension and trouble. Otherwise you turn against nature. In group process, recall that sunshine follows rain. Remember water, wind. Be aware that the leader in you follows a plan, but the elder follows a mysterious and unknown river.

9. Parent the chaos, don't kill the fire. Every group needs to process its atmosphere regularly, at every season, at least four times a year. Every group process deals with the world's great, unsolved problems. Whether the group is small or huge, group problems are always global. They are monumental. Parent the chaos. Accept periods of confusion and disorder. Don't kill the fire. Acknowledge the heat. Sit in the fire of community with everyone who is able to process issues and emotions.

10. Begin. That's it: simply begin. Realize that you don't have to push to get going; it's already happening. Just wake up to your next breath, next interaction, next meeting, next group.

Tell folks if you feel unfree around them. Show how they use rank unconsciously. When they complain about your behavior, congratulate them for looking closely at you. Stand for your views. Or show how you, too, can be unconscious of rank, or use your knowledge and awareness unwisely. That's eldership. It's standing up and being strong, accepting weakness, modeling in public how to discover your own unconsciousness while still respecting yourself and others. It's process, not perfection, which counts in nature.

Enlightenment accepts unconsciousness as a temporary part of the flow. The way human history proceeds can change only if we use our awareness to process issues instead of trying to eradicate unconsciousness, authority figures and all "bad" things.

What is true of Soto Zen is also true of deep democracy: enlightenment arises from awareness of how you travel the path, not through the attainment of a permanent goal.

Individuals have always sought enlightenment. Why not groups? All that's necessary is for groups to become aware of their process instead of trying to kill it. We kill people, but we cannot do away with the ranks or roles they stand for. Economic injustice does not disappear with new social laws. You cannot do away with those who steal money. You cannot do away with those who commit adultery, take drugs or fulfill their private interests at the expense of public needs. You have to bring behavior forward, admit it, try to process it, debate it, make it useful, fight against it. With such an attitude, you'll find that trouble is the best way to community.

WARNING: DEMOCRACY AHEAD!

Killing oppressors is oppressive, but don't expect that to stop, either. The talionic law says there is no way around revenge; you get back what you give. That law governs history.

The leaders of the Russian Revolution thought that the masses needed re-education. But when they forced this education, they unwittingly used against the masses the ghost role they had projected onto the czar. The hippies, members of a student movement in Europe and the United States in the 1960s, were similar. That isn't surprising, since they drew inspiration from such communist thinkers as Rosa Luxemburg, Trotsky and Sinnoviev, who believed that anyone affected by a decision must have access to the place where decisions are made and to the decision-makers.[2] The hippies insisted that they vote on everything that concerned them. They insisted on being present when every university decision was made. Following Luxemburg, Trotsky and Sinnoviev, they did not act on the basis of what the majority wanted; their idea was to work for consensus and to sit until the whole group was behind what was decided. They rejected parliamentary democracy. They refused to be represented by a delegate.

This sounds great. But finally, the hippies were as repressive as dictators. Like some of their models, such as the most extreme Soviet leaders, they were so radically democratic that they became repressive to anyone who wanted to take a strong hand in things. "Bad" people are not the worst problem — our methods of dealing with them through law, repression, forced "education" and, above all, the assumption they must change are worse. Beware of the democracies of the future. Without heightened consciousness, they will not be revolutions; they will barely be reforms.

THE BASICS OF REVOLUTION

The stage is set for another revolution. Consider these elements that contribute to a revolution and ask yourself whether they exist today in your group or in the world:[3]

Mass frustration. Think of the millions of the proletariat who were negated, neglected and abused by the Czar before 1917. That led to revolution. Is there mass frustration today? I would call the frustration with world problems almost global.

Help for the revolution from the top or support from dissident elite. Some of those in power who have not been recognized stand behind the masses. For example, academics played important roles in the earliest communist revolutions. There are many such people today in many governments, including the United Nations (UN).

Great visions and high goals — unifying motivations that cut across class and unite people in the struggle for liberation. This was the case, for example, in Vietnam, where a population inspired by nationalism pulled together against the French and later against the United States. Do we have visions today that cut across classes and nations? Yes, elements in our religious tradition, indigenous thinking and modern theories are truly global.

Failure of the governing powers. Sometimes revolutionary crisis is supported by catastrophes, failure in war, economic depression or the withdrawal of outside support. Revolution, for example, was made possible in the Soviet Union in the late 1980s because the government was economically depressed and unable to support itself. The earthquake that shook Managua in 1972 weakened the government and proved to be a precursor of revolution. Threat of destruction from outside or within lays the groundwork for revolution. Do such conditions exist today? Yes. The super powers are collapsing. We are inundated by news reports about the failure of governments.

Support from the outside. Revolution is made easier if other groups or countries do not intervene to prevent radical change. Because neither Russia nor the United States intervened, revolutions went forward in many Eastern European countries in the late 1980s and early 1990s. Supportive, or at least passive, outer relationships facilitate sudden changes within communities.

ELDERS OUTSIDE THE WORLD

Here is a problem for our global village: no one is outside the world. All the other factors that could precipitate a world revolution are in place. A huge change in consciousness could occur. Democracy is not working.

But we have too few Buddhas sitting outside the wheel of life and death. Where are the elders who are both outside and in? We need you to become an elder with multicultural training and a meta-view, to sit in the fire and not get burned. Revolution can't really begin without a support "outside," that is, without eldership.

President Vaclav Havel, the dissident playwright whose spirit inspired the Czechs through the revolution, stood before the United States Congress in 1990 and said it clearly. "Without a

global revolution in the sphere of human consciousness, a more
humane society will not emerge."

But he did not say we are missing the eldership to manage
the change we need. This lack of multicultural eldership leaves
us, at the turn of the third millennium, scarcely at the point of
reform in deep democracy, much less real revolution.

The first step toward revolution in the sphere of human consciousness is the biggest one — you, risking being an elder and
facilitating group processes. Get into the heat. Make up your own
ten steps. This immediate goal is all that we need to realize.

History is not an abstract event that happens to others. History is how you facilitate, how you live your day-to-day personal
and group processes.

THINKING YOU CAN'T MAKE A DIFFERENCE IS JUST AN EDGE

If you need encouragement, remember the Civil Rights and Anti-
War movements in the United States during the 1960s. They left
many changes still to be made but showed us that the gigantic
apparatus of government could be induced to alter its policies
fast. What it took was individuals and small groups who were
committed enough to risk going to jail. The activists who were
willing to be imprisoned for social change when all negotiations
failed demonstrated that small numbers of people with moral
determination and a willingness to sacrifice can make big
changes. Remember the Blacks in Alabama and South Africa; the
peasants of El Salvador, Nicaragua and Vietnam; the workers
and intellectuals in Eastern Europe and the Soviet Union.

The lesson is that individuals alone or banding together can
make a quantum leap for the rest of the world. Don't dismiss
what we as individuals can do because we are only several in a
sea of millions. Feeling you can't change the world is just another
edge, one you can get over.

THE POLITICS OF AWARENESS

Thinking globally gives you perspective on our needs. Consider
that if the lure of nationalism continues, by the year 2010 there
could be as many as three hundred separate nation states. In the
past several years, the number of large military conflicts taking
place simultaneously around the world has increased from 32 to

40. As a result, 40 million people are refugees. By the year 2000, the number of refugees may exceed 100 million.

Our international political system is not working; it's time for something new. We need a politics of awareness that will support deep democracy, which is neither conservative nor liberal. It could even mean the end of our obsessing about the support or downfall of capitalism or socialism. It would mean clarity about rank and greed. This new politics would do more than ruminate righteously on how one power takes over another. It would look at how conflict transforms them both.

MULTICULTURALISM

A politics of awareness supports multicultural studies and culture-centric viewpoints. In the United States, for example, this means supporting the Native American, African, Latino, Japanese, Chinese, Islamic, Jewish, Christian, transpersonal, atheistic and many more viewpoints — not submerging them in a melting pot that turns out to be mainstream Eurocentric.

Polarity is the basis of awareness. We need to do more than read textbooks about one another. We need places where we can meet, debate, have it out, get into emotional states and use our awareness. We need a place to dream together, to get into what has been kept unknown. Dreaming means flowing with the unknown river of community.

This new politics creates a place for the unknown, for anger, vengefulness, love and insight. Multicultural life means encouraging deep subgroup experiences as well as all-community experience. It means warming up frozen and rigid opinions and attitudes to the point at which they combine and recombine.

THE FIELD APPROACH: EVERYTHING ABOUT EVERYONE COUNTS

In the new paradigm, you are the leader, the government, the boss, the facilitator, the criminal, the savior and the dreamer. It's not always someone else, it's you. At various times, you have to step in and play all of those roles.

Every one of us senses that the big problems are so interconnected that the only way to address them is the field approach. From the viewpoint of a field, citizens are not only objects capable of power and voting. They are individuals and unique expressions of the community. Everything about everyone counts.

The field leads. You can facilitate. Issues, domination, oppression, feelings and dreams are important, too. They are not merely obstacles on the path for you or your group to overcome before you can make progress. Just facing them is the progress.

If you are in the role of leader, expect to be attacked. Remember, other people are upset not only by what you do, but because you have a role valued by society. When you are accused of something, step forward, bring it out on TV, model for your people and country how relationship work can go. Invite your attackers to join you. Then, win or lose, you are a leader graduating into eldership.

BODIES AND BEHAVIORS EXPRESS WORLD ENERGIES

In the new politics, social awareness relieves health issues. Many illnesses are not curable now because modern medicine is based on pathology — cause, effect and cure. Our illnesses are not just pathological. They are not only enemies but potential allies. They are expressions of world energies, timespirits, processes.

An illness is not a terrorist to be killed with antibiotics. A headache cannot be cured by aspirin alone, but by gaining access to the pounding energies that want something new in life. Your body reacts to the world. You need to know the body from the inside out. Then you realize it is like the world, full of trouble and timespirits asking for interaction.

The politics of awareness encourages less spending on medicine and more on the incredible personal power embedded in symptoms; less on politics and the military and more on learning about double edges; less on law and the media and more in understanding the psychology of war.

This will reduce the number of criminals, increase the number of people whose voices will be appreciated — and reduce the number of ambulances we need to pick up those who have been shot!

Legal actions against the "evil" ones, citizen review boards, money spent to desegregate, crime surveys and jails are part of the old democracy. Legal action in adversarial systems exacerbates problems by ignoring the relationship between the criminal and the community. In the new paradigm, crime is a community problem. The problems are not only in the hot spots in those cities and nations where murder is rampant. In the new paradigm, the criminal is a timespirit at war with the status quo of the majority. The criminal is not a person who is "evil" and deserving of punishment, but an all-pervasive spirit. This could mean the end of almost all prisons.

The best advice for nations and cities is to give first priority to government spending that encourages ongoing study of how we get along with one another. Wise politicians would promote innerwork, relationship work and social awareness. Without these, our physical health is endangered by tension, our everyday lives are invaded by crime and war, and the national economy crumbles as military spending soars to protect us against neighbors.

LEADERS WHO MODEL REVOLUTION

Government in the new paradigm is a misnomer, because the real government is the process of the people and the environment. "Leaders" get smaller. They are ordinary people who happen to be better than others at public speaking. Our present "leaders" under capitalism have more marketing strategies than relationship skills. The new leaders will be elders who appear in the media and work in the open on their relationship problems with citizens. Their problems will support change in all of us.

Teachers will model awareness in our new world. In our present alternative teaching systems, teachers try to minimize their power in order to create equality in the classroom. They empower students. In the new politics of awareness, teachers are neither authoritarian nor humble. They stand for their rank and notice what's happening. They encourage others to focus on process as well as content. They model revolution by standing firmly. At other times, they invite criticism and group process. It's easy. All of us should have learned about group process in kindergarten. Our lives would be more fun today.

WHOLENESS IS OPENNESS TO WHAT'S HAPPENING

What will change in your day-by-day experience depends on you as an individual. Certain aspects of life can be predicted, though.

Education and therapy, which have been puppets of social unconsciousness, will no longer tout integration into the mainstream as the great goal. They will no longer blind people to the social and political factors that are formative of our inner life. Psychologists will recognize that innerwork cannot be separated from the trends of history. Amy Mindell discusses how this can be done in her article "The World Channel."[4] Feminists and social psychologists have recognized for years the connection between inner oppression and outer political domination. They began a revolution in which this consciousness will lead to a sense of liberation.

Service to the world will take on new dimensions. Religious and spiritual teachers such as Christ and Buddha, modern people such as Gandhi, Martin Luther King and the Dalai Lama, and many religious groups have contributed to our understanding of the connection between spiritual attainment and worldly service. Liberation theology stresses service based on an understanding of history and the liberation of the oppressed, integrating the sense of inner freedom with socio-political liberation.

Now service to the world will also be a form of innerwork that sees the connections between inner states and the outer atmosphere. Innerwork becomes worldwork when you notice how your dreams connect with issues of rank and roles, race, gender, violence, women's rights, war, nuclear threats and ecology. As the healing community itself recuperates from its focus on the individual independent of the world, therapy and politics will come together, both of them committed to the health of the larger political body and the environment.

Wholeness will mean openness to what is happening at the moment, not some once-and-for-all integration of your inner parts. Wholeness will mean clarity about outer diversity. It means field awareness, noticing oppressors, victims and healers. Awareness stops us from putting halos on victims. In the next moment, that victim can be an oppressor on another issue. Gone are the days of permanently separating racism, sexism, homophobia, ageism and other issues from one another.

Wholeness could be really exciting. We will be present in the workplace not only as money-earners, but as real people, as roles, as citizens of our town, state, nation, and the world, supporters of the environment, including the psychological and spiritual environments that so profoundly affect our spirits. We will be involved in how our company invests its money and utilizes the time it has to give to the community. We will insist that the business is itself a member of the community, that business prospers only if the community does, that the barometer of its success is not dollars but its vitality as an organ in the larger social body. Best of all, we will get bored with making only those on top the evil ones. Given the chance, we know we can be just as evil.

At home, children will be respected in their rank as children. Parents will be aware of their rank and realize when they misuse it. Everyone will be encouraged to go deeper into feelings, roles and issues of freedom, authority, love and independence. No longer will there be one person in the role of neglecting the kids and the other in the role of the good parent. Everyone is in all the roles. Family therapists will love this; they have recommended it for a long time.

The extended family will not mean only uncles and aunts, but the entire environment — rocks and rivers, plants, animals and every human being. Families will honor their dead and all humans who have lived before us. Everybody counts. History is present, watching, participating.

From The Shamanic Circle To Worldwork: A Small Step

Perhaps we are all one family. Some scientists claim that we originated in East Africa, where the earliest form of humans has been found. Wherever our ancestors came from, there was a time when they lived in small groups and were united by the spirit of shamanism, their shared sense of mystery, their spirit ancestors, their totems and their rituals for birth, puberty, marriage, hunting, planting, harvesting and death. All of us, through our dreams, were the common ground guiding the community. Shamans saw each individual as a role in the tribal field. That field existed within each individual. Healing was done in a circle. Shamanic dreaming is our common past.

In the politics of awareness, we recapture some of these fertile, dynamic properties of community. What we currently lack in society, that old-time numinous experience of people together, can be found in the very thing we fear the most: large groups, masses of people feeling deeply about things. The spirits in such groups can be the creativity, the dance, the sense of community we long for.

There's little difference between the old tribal circle where shamans and tribespeople went into altered states of consciousness and worldwork in which marginal processes are brought up and people become afraid and excited. The vocabulary has changed but the processes are basically the same. Speak of demons, secondary processes, ghosts or government, community process will always be full of impossible timespirits and people. It may include athletes or city leaders, hunters or business people, ecstatics or advertisers, oppressors or victims. Community is dreaming together. It is the evening news, Sunday morning prayer and everybody's visions.

There is one important difference between worldwork and tribal life. Tribal people speak unselfconsciously about the dynamics of spiritual process. The Desanas, Hopis, Kyukons, Dunne-zas, Chewong and aboriginal Australians say our job is to connect to powers that were never ours, to witness and use them to help the atmosphere we live in.

Few who participate in Western Civilization realize that the evening news is full of timespirits and dreaming. Soon such thinking will be common, though. No city, state or government will survive without the metaskill of benevolence to the dreaming, ongoing process.

MAKE PEACE WITH WAR

The world themes that separate us today are the struggle for physical survival, concern for our planet's ecology, the war against oppression, the longing for freedom and equality, the need to overcome every kind of prejudice, and the sense of being valuable and powerful. My experiences with thousands of people demonstrate that all our conflicts, differences and issues, oppressions and prejudices, unconsciousness and power struggles — the very themes that separate us — if suffered through to an awakening, draw us together.

Organizations and communities do not fail because of their problems, nor do they necessarily succeed because they solve them. Problems will always exist. Communities that succeed open up to the unknown during periods of crisis. We succeed in the grand sense and become sustainable by following the cycle of things. We come together by following the flow — through operating as a community, having trouble, almost going to pieces and then coming together. Such organizations live forever. They can't die. They are the Tao, always changing.

You don't have to go far to begin dreaming or meet with timespirits. They are one breath away. What you are feeling right now is the point; it's a timespirit. Your feelings are needed to make the community complete.

The world is composed of our individual experiences. It is the relationship process between the two of us, among the hundreds of us, among the millions of us. The world is the joy, the mess, the chaos that sweeps us up during times of trouble. Managed with love, things can change quickly. Leaders step back as the elders come out. They too melt into the group, which itself takes over.

To make this a better world, notice the timespirits and bring them forward. Then you are doing individual work, relationship work and worldwork in one. Value trouble. Accept nature. Make peace with war. Fewer people will be hurt. Enjoy the sunshine and the rain, and nature will do the rest.

That's the revolution we need.

Notes

1. See Defronzo, *Revolution and Revolutionary Movements*, pp. 10-15, which I largely follow in the ideas presented here about reform and revolution.
2. See Anne Strick, *Injustice for All*.
3. Again after Defronzo, op. cit.
4. Mindell, Amy. "The World Channel in Individual Work," *The Journal of Process Oriented Psychology*, Vol. 5, No. 1.

Bibliography

BOOKS & ARTICLES

Acuña, Rodolfo. *Occupied America: A History of Chicanos.* NY: Harper-Collins, 3rd ed., 1988.

Adler, Nancy. *International Dimensions of Organizational Behavior.* Boston: PWS-Kent Publishing, 2nd ed., 1991.

Administrative Conference of the United States Sourcebook. Federal Agency Use of Alternative Means of Dispute Resolution, June, 1987.

Almanac. *The 1992 Information Please Almanac.* Boston: Houghton Mifflin Co., 1992.

American Medical Association Encyclopedia of Medicine. NY: Random House, 1989.

Anderson, W. "Politics and the new humanism." *Journal of Humanistic Psychology,* 1974, 14(4), pp. 5-27.

Ani, Marimba. *Yurugu: An African-Centered Critique of European Cultural Thought and Behavior.* NY and Trenton: The African World Press, 1994.

Bayer, C. "Politics and Pilgrimages." *Pilgrimage: Journal of Psychotherapy and Personal Exploration.* Jan/Feb, 1990. 16, 1.

de Beauvoir, Simone. *The Second Sex.* NY: Vintage Books, 1974.

Berry, Wendell. *What Are People For: Essays*. San Francisco: North Point Press, 1990.

Bloch, D. (1994) Afterword. In *The Global Family Therapist: Integrating the Personal, Professional and Political*. B.B. Gould and D.H. DeMuth, eds. Boston: Allyn and Bacon, pp. 281-284.

Boyd-Franklin, N. "Pulling Out The Arrows." *The Family Therapy Networker*, July/August, 1993, pp. 55-56.

Buber, M. *I and Thou*. NY: Charles Scribner, 1970.

Bugental, J. "The Humanistic Ethic: The Individual in Psychotherapy as a Societal Change Agent." *Journal of Humanistic Psychology*. Spring, 1971, 11(7), pp. 11-25.

Burton, John. *Conflict: Resolution and Provention*. NY: St. Martin's Press, 1990.

Capra, F. "Modern Physics and Eastern Mysticism." *Beyond Ego: Transpersonal Dimensions in Psychology*, R.N. Walsh and F. Vaughn, eds. Los Angeles: Tarcher, 1980.

Collinson, D. *Fifty Major Philosophers: A Reference Guide*. London and NY: Croom Helm, 1987.

Chen, Ellen. *Tao Te Ching*. NY: Paragon House, 1989.

Chessler, Phyllis. *Women and Madness: A History of Women and the Psychiatric Profession*. NY: Doubleday, 1972.

Chomsky, Noam. *Year 501: The Conquest Continues*. Boston, South End Press, 1993.

Cohen, Carl. *Democracy*. NY: The Free Press, 1971.

Crumb, Thomas. *The Magic of Conflict: Turning a Life of Work into a Work of Art*. NY: Touchstone/Simon and Schuster, 1987.

Defronzo, James. *Revolutions and Revolutionary Movements*. Boulder, CO: Westview Press, 1991.

Demause, Lloyd. *Foundations of Psychohistory*. NY: Creative Roots, 1982.

Devall, B. and Sessions, G. "Deep Ecology: Living As If Nature Mattered." *Paths Beyond Ego: The Transpersonal Vision*, R.N. Walsh and Frances Vaughan, eds. Los Angeles: Tarcher, 1993.

Dreifus, C. *Women's Fate*. NY: Bantam Books, 1993.

Diamond, Julie. "A Process-Oriented Study on Sexuality and Homosexuality." Portland, OR: Work in progress at the Process Work Center of Portland.

di Leonardo, Maeaela. "Racial Fairy Tales." *The Nation*, Dec. 9, 1991.

Donnelly, Jack. "Human Rights in the New World Order." *World Policy Journal*, Spring, 1992.

Dworkin, J. "Group Process Work: A Stage for Personal and Global Development." Diss. Union Institute, 1989.

Ehrenreich, Barbara and English, Deirdre. *For Her Own Good: 150 Years of the Experts' Advice to Women*. NY: Anchor Books, 1978.

Einstein, Albert. *The Meaning of Relativity*. Princeton, NJ: Princeton University Press, 1922.

Eisler, Riane. *The Chalice and the Blade: Our History, Our Future.* NY: Harper & Row, 1987.

Elgin, D. "The Tao of Personal and Social Transformation." *Beyond Ego: Transpersonal Dimensions In Psychology.* R.N. Walsh & F. Vaughan. eds. Los Angeles: Tarcher, 1980.

Elliot, Dorinda and LeVine, Steve. "An Ethnic Nightmare in the Caucasus." *Newsweek,* Dec. 7, 1992.

Emetchi, J.M. "Between the Sheets of Power: Feminist Bisexuality Revisited." Portland, OR: Special Study at Portland State University and the Process Work Center, Portland, Oregon, 1995.

Ettinger, Elzbieta, ed. *Comrade and Lover: Rosa Luxemburg's Letters to Leo Jogishes.* Cambridge, MA: MIT Press, 1979.

Etzioni, Amitai. *The Spirit of Community: Rights, Responsibilities, and the Communitarian Agenda.* NY: Crown Publishers, 1993.

Ewing, Blaire. "Letters to the Editor." *Yoga Journal,* Jan., 1993.

Fanon, Frantz. *The Wretched of the Earth.* NY: Grove Press, 1965.

Fox, W. "Transpersonal Ecology." *Paths Beyond Ego: The Transpersonal Vision.* R.N. Walsh and F. Vaughan, eds. Los Angeles: Tarcher, 1993.

Franklin, A.J. "The Invisibility Syndrome." *The Family Therapy Networker,* July/August, 1993.

Friedman, M. *Revealing and Obscuring the Human.* Pittsburg: Duquesne University Press, 1984.

Freire, P. *Pedagogy in Process.* NY: Seabury, 1978.

——— . *Pedagogy of the Oppressed.* NY: Continuum, 1992.

Freud, Sigmund. *The Basic Writings of Sigmund Freud.* A. A. Brill, trans. NY: Modern Library, 1938.

Frey, R. G., and Morris, Christopher W., eds. *Violence, Terrorism and Justice.* NY: Cambridge University Press, 1991.

Fromkim, David. "The Coming Millennium, World Politics in the Twenty-First Century." *World Policy Journal,* Spring, 1993, X: 1.

Fukuyama, Francis. "Liberal Democracy as a Global Phenomena." *PS: Political Science and Politics* 34:4, Dec., 1991.

——— . "The Future in Their Past." *The Economist,* Nov., 1992.

Galtung, Johan. *Peace and Social Structure: Essays in Peace Research,* Volume Three. Copenhagen: Christian Ejliers, 1978.

Gay, Peter. *Freud for Historians.* NY: Oxford University Press, 1985.

Glauser, Benno. *In The Streets: Working Street Children in Asuncion.* Susana Cahill, trans. NY: UNICEF, Methodological Series, Regional Programme, "Children in Especially Difficult Circumstances," No. 4, 1988.

Gomes, Mary E. "The Rewards and Stresses of Social Change: A Qualitative Study of Peace Activists." *The Journal of Humanistic Psychology,* 32:4, Fall, 1992.

Goodway, David. *For Anarchism, History, Theory and Practice*. London and NY: Routledge, 1989.

Gould, B.B. & DeMuth, D.H., eds. *The Global Family Therapist: Integrating the Personal, Professional, and Political*. Boston: Allyn and Bacon, 1994.

Greening, T., ed. *American Politics and Humanistic Psychology*. Dallas: Saybrook Institute Press, 1984.

Gurtov, M. *Making Changes: The Politics of Self-Liberation*. Oakland, CA: Harvest Moon Books, 1979.

Gutierrez, Gustavo. *A Theology of Liberation: History, Politics and Salvation*. NY: Orbis Books, 1988.

Hacker, Andrew. *Two Nations: Black and White, Separate, Hostile, Unequal*. NY: Scribner's, 1992.

Halprin, Sara.*"Look at my Ugly Face!": Myths and Muslins on Beauty and Other Perilous Obsessions With Women's Appearance*. New York/London: Viking Penguin, 1995.

———. "Talking About Our Lives and Experiences: Some Thoughts About Feminism, Documentary, and 'Talking Heads.'" *Show Us Life: Towards a History and Aesthetics of the Committed Documentary*. Tomas Waugh, ed. Metuchen, NJ: Scarecrow Press, 1984.

Nhat-Hanh, Thich. *Touching Peace: The Art of Mindful Living*. Berkeley, CA: Parallax Press, 1991.

———. *Peace is Every Step: The Path of Mindfulness in Everyday Life*. Berkeley, CA: Parallax Press, 1992.

Hardy, K. "War of the Worlds." *The Family Therapy Networker*, July/August, 1993.

Harner, Michael. *The Way of the Shaman*. NY: Bantam Books, 1986.

Held, David. *Models of Democracy: From Athenian Democracy to Marx*. CA: Stanford University Press, 1987.

Herman, Judith. *Trauma and Recovery*. NY: Basic Books, 1992.

Hillman, James and Ventura, Michael. *We've Had A Hundred Years of Psychotherapy and the World's Getting Worse*. San Francisco: HarperSanFrancisco, 1993.

Hollander, E.P. & Hunt, R.G., eds. *Classic Contributions of Social Psychology*. London and Toronto: Oxford University Press, 1972.

Hooks, Bell. *Sisters of the Yam: Black Women and Self-Recovery*. Boston: South End Press, 1993.

Horsman, Reginald. *Race and Manifest Destiny*. Boston: Harvard University Press, 1981.

Hugo, Victor. *Les Miserables*. NY: Fawcett Books, 1987.

Ingram. Catherine. *In the Footsteps of Gandhi: Conversations with Spiritual Social Activists*. Berkeley, CA: Parallax Press, 1990.

Jordan, June. *Technical Difficulties*. NY: Pantheon Books, 1992.

Jorns, A. *The Quakers as Pioneers in Social Work*. Port Washington, WA: Kennikat Press, Inc., 1931.

Jung, C.G. *Contributions to Analytical Psychology*. NY: Harcourt, Brace, 1928.

——. "Your Negroid And Indian Behavior." *Forum*, 83, 1930.

——. "Psychological Types," *The Complete Works*, Vol. 6. Princeton, NJ: Princeton University Press, 1966.

——. *The Undiscovered Self*. Boston: Little, Brown, 1958.

Kaplan, Lawrence and Carol. *Revolutions: A Comparative Study from Cromwell to Castro*. NY: Vintage Books, 1973.

Kelly, Kevin. "Chilling Scenarios for the Post Cold War World." *Utne Reader*, Sept/Oct, 1993.

Kim, Nam H., Song-Won Sohn, Jay S., and Wall, James A. "Community and Industrial Mediation in South Korea." *Journal of Conflict Resolution*, 37: 2, June, 1993.

King, Jr., Martin Luther. *I Have a Dream: Writings and Speeches that Changed the World*. San Francisco: Harper SanFrancisco, 1992.

Kochman, Thomas. *Black and White Styles in Conflict*. IL: University of Chicago Press, 1983.

Kohut, Heinz. *Self-Psychology and the Humanistic: Reflections on a Psychoanalytic Approach*. NY: W.W. Norton, 1985.

Knudtson, Peter and Suzuki, David. *The Wisdom of the Elders*. Toronto: Allen and Unwin, 1992.

Korzenny, Felipe and Ting-Toomey, Stella. *Communicating for Peace, Diplomacy and Negotiation: A Multicultural Exploration of How Culture Affects Peace Negotiations*. Newbury Park, CA: Sage Publications, Inc., 1990.

Kozol, Jonathon. *Savage Inequalities: Children in America's Schools*. NY: Harper & Row, 1992.

Laing, R.D. *The Divided Self: An Existential Study in Sanity and Madness*. NY: Penguin Books, 1965.

Lafferty, J. "Political Responsibility and the Human Potential Movement." *Journal of Humanistic Psychology*, 21: 1, 1981.

Lao-Tzu. *Tao Te Ching*. Trans. Gia-fu Feng and Jane English. New York: Vintage Books, 1972.

Lao-Tzu. *Tao Te Ching, The Book of Meaning and Life*. Trans. from Chinese into German, Richard Wilhelm. Trans. into English by H. G. Ostwald. London/New York: Viking-Penguin-Arkana, 1985.

Lawlor, Robert. *Voices of the First Day: Awakening in the Aboriginal Dreamtime*. Rochester, VT: Inner Traditions International, 1991.

Lewin, K. "Need, Force and Valence in Psychological Fields" in *Classic Contributions to Social Psychology*. E.P. Hollander and R.G. Hunt, eds. London: Oxford University Press, 1972.

Lovelock, J. E. *Gaia: A New Look at LIfe on Earth*. London and NY: Oxford University Press, 1979.

Mack, J. E. and Redmont, J., "On Being a Psychoanalyst in the Nuclear Age." *Journal of Humanistic Psychology,* 29: 3, 1989.

Macy, Joanna. *Despair and Personal Power in the Nuclear Age.* Philadelphia: New Society Publishers, 1983.

———. *World as Lover, World as Self.* Berkeley, CA: Parallax Press, 1991.

Mahesh, V. S. *The Corporation as Nursery for Human Growth.* NY: McGraw-Hill, 1993.

Maltz, Wendy. *The Sexual Healing Journey: A Guide for Survivors of Sexual Abuse.* NY: Harper & Row, 1992.

Mao, Tse-Tung. *Selected Military Writing.* Peking: Foreign Languages Press, 1963.

Malcolm X Speaks. NY: Pathfinder, 1989.

———. *Selected Speeches and Statements of Malcolm X.* NY: Grove Press, 1990.

———. *Malcolm X: Speeches.* NY: Pathfinder, 1992.

———. *The Autobiography of Malcolm X.* NY: Ballantine Books, 1965.

Marx, Karl. *Grundrisse Der Kritik der Politischen Oekonomie, 1857-1858.* Berlin/Frankfurt: Europaiesche Verlag, 1967.

———. "Communist Manifesto." *Karl Marx and Frederick Engels: Selected Works.* NY: International Publishers, 1968.

———. "Critiques of the Goethe Programme." *Karl Marx: Selected Writings in Sociology and Social Philosophy.* T. B. Bottomore, ed. and trans. NY: McGraw-Hill, 1956.

———. *Portable Karl Marx.* Eugene Kamenka, ed. NY: Penguin, 1983.

Masey, Douglas and Denton, Nancy. *American Apartheid: Segregation and the Making of the Underclass.* Cambridge, MA: Harvard University Press, 1993.

Maslow, Abraham. *Toward a Psychology of Being.* NY: Van Nostrand, 1968.

———. *The Farther Reaches of Human Nature.* NY: Viking, 1971.

McDonald, Eileen. *Shoot the Women First.* NY: Random House, 1991.

McWilliams, Wayne, and Piotrowski, Harry. *The World Since 1945: A History of International Relations.* Boulder, CO, and London: Lynne Rienner Publishers, 1993.

Medecins Sans Frontiers, *Populations in Danger.* Francois Jean, ed. London: John Libbey & Co., 1992.

Mindell, Amy. "The World Channel in Individual Work." *Journal of Process-Oriented Psychology,* Vol. 5, No.1, 1993.

———. "Discovering the World in the Individual: The Worldchannel in Psychotherapy." *Journal of Humanistic Psychology,* 1995.

———. *Metaskills: The Spiritual Art of Therapy.* Santa Monica, CA: New Falcon Press, 1995.

———. *Riding the Horse Backwards: Process Work in Theory and Practice with Arny Mindell.* NY: Penguin Books, 1992.

Mindell, Arnold. *Working with the Dreaming Body*. NY and London: Penguin-Arkana, 1984.

—— . *River's Way: The Process Science of the Dreambody*. NY and London: Viking-Penguin-Arkana, 1986.

—— . *The Dreambody in Relationships*. NY and London: Viking-Penguin-Arkana, 1987.

—— . *City Shadows: Psychological Interventions Psychiatry*. NY and London: Viking-Penguin-Arkana, 1988.

—— . *Inner Dreambodywork: Working on Yourself Alone*. NY and London: Viking-Penguin-Arkana, 1990.

—— . *The Year 1: Global Process Work with Planetary Tensions*. NY and London: Viking-Penguin-Arkana, 1990.

—— . *The Leader as Martial Artist: An Introduction to Deep Democracy, Techniques and Strategies for Resolving Conflict and Creating Community*. San Francisco: HarperCollins, 1992.

—— . *The Shaman's Body*. San Francisco: HarperCollins, 1993.

Mindell, Carl. "Shaming." Lecture at Albany Medical School. NY: 1992.

Mura, David. "Whites: How To Face The Angry Racial Tribes." *Utne Reader*, July/Aug, 1992.

Muwakkil, Salim. "In These Times." *Utne Reader*, July/Aug, 1992.

Naison, Mark. An editorial in *Reconstruction*, I: 4, 1992.

Neihardt, John G. *Black Elk Speaks: Being the Life Story of a Holy Man of the Oglala Sioux*. NY: Simon and Schuster, 1972.

New English Bible with the Apocrypha. NY: Penguin Books, 1970.

O'Brien, Mark and Little, Craig, eds. *The Arts of Social Change*. Santa Cruz, CA: New Society Publishers, 1990.

Owen, Harrison. *Open Space Technology: A User's Guide*. Potomac, MD: Abbott, 1992.

Parry, Danaan. *Warriors of the Heart*. Cooperstown, NY: Sunstone Publications, 1991.

Pasternak, Boris. *Dr. Zhivago*. NY: Knopf, 1991.

Pate, Alex. *Losing Absalom*. Minneapolis, MN: Coffee House Press, 1993.

Peck, M. Scott. *A Different Drum: Community Making and Peace*. NY: Simon and Schuster, 1987.

Pepper, Stephen C. *World Hypotheses*. Berkeley: University of California Press, 1961.

Prigogine, Ilya. *From Being to Becoming*. San Francisco: Freeman, 1980.

—— . *Order Out of Chaos*. NY: Bantam, 1984.

Ravitch, Diance and Thernstrom, Abigail, eds. *The Democracy Reader: Classic and Modern Speeches, Essays, Poems, Declarations, and Documents on Freedom and Human Rights Worldwide*. NY: Harper Perennial, 1992.

Reagon, Bernice Johnson. The foreword to *Reimaging America: The Arts of Social Change*. Craig Little and Mark O'Brian, eds. Philadelphia: New Society Publications, 1990.

Rinpoche, Sogyal. *The Tibetan Book of Living and Dying*. San Francisco: HarperCollins, 1992.

Rourke, J. T., Hiskes, R. P., and Zirakzadeh, C. E. *Direct Democracy and International Politics: Deciding International Issues Through Referendums*. Boulder, CO, and London: Lynne Rienner Publishers, 1992.

Rozak, Theodore. *The Voice of the Earth*. NY: Simon and Schuster, 1992.

——— . "The Greening of Psychology." *Ecopsychology Newsletter*. Spring, 1994.

Rogers, C.R. *A Way of Being*. Boston: Houghton Mifflin Co., 1980.

——— . *Carl Rogers on Personal Power: Inner Strength and its Revolutionary Impact*. NY: Dell Publishing Company. Inc., 1977.

Rummel, R. J. "The Politics Of Cold Blood." *Society*, Nov/Dec, 1989.

Rush, Florence. *The Best Kept Secret: Sexual Abuse of Children*. NY: McGraw-Hill, 1981.

Sakharov, Andre. *Memoirs*. NY: Knopf, 1992.

Samuels, A. *The Political Psyche*. London and NY: Routledge, 1993.

Szasz, T. *Law, Liberty, and Psychiatry*. NY: Macmillan, 1963.

Schur, E. *The Awareness Trap: Self-Absorption Instead of Social Change*. NY: Quandrangle/The New York Times Book Co., 1976.

Schumpeter, Joseph. *Capitalism, Socialism, and Democracy*. London: Allen and Unwin, 1943.

Seed, John. "An Interview With John Seed And Ram Dass." *The Sun*, Jan., 1993.

Shevardnadze, Eduard. "1992 Address to the Georgian Parliament." Brochure by the Georgian Parliament, Jan., 1993.

Sipe, Robert. "Dialectic and Method: Reconstructing Radical Therapy." *The Journal of Humanistic Psychology*, 26: 2 Spring, 1986.

Singer, June. "Culture and the Collective Unconscious." Diss. Northwestern University, 1968.

Skerry, Peter. *Mexican Americans: The Ambivalent Minority*. NY and Toronto: Free Press, 1993.

Skocpol, Theda. *States and Social Revolutions: A Comparative Analysis of France, Russia and China*. NY: Cambridge University Press, 1990.

Small, Melvin and Singer, J. David. "The War-Proneness of Democratic Regimes, 1816-1965." *Jerusalem Journal of International Relationship*, 1976.

Spence, Jo. *Putting Myself in the Picture: A Political, Personal and Photographic Autobiography*. Seattle: The Real Comet Press, 1986.

Strick, Anne. *Injustice for All*. NY: G. P. Putnam, 1977.

Suzuki, David and Knudtson, Peter. *The Wisdom of the Elders*. Toronto: Allen and Unwin, 1992.

Terkel, Studs. *How Blacks and Whites Think and Feel about Race: The American Obsession*. NY: The New Press, 1992.

Thomas, Alexander, and Sillen, Samuel. *Racism and Psychiatry*. NY: New Press, 1983.

Vassiliou, Alexandra, "Listen or Die: the Terrorist as a Role." Diss. Union Institute, 1995.

Walsh, R. and Vaughan, F., eds. *Paths Beyond Ego: The Transpersonal Vision*. Los Angeles: Jeremy P. Tarcher, 1993.

———. *Beyond Ego: Transpersonal Dimensions in Psychology*. Los Angeles: Jeremy P. Tarcher, Inc., 1980.

Watzlawick, P., Beavin, J., and Jackson, D. *Pragmatics of Human Communication: A Study of Interactional Patterns, Pathologies and Paradoxes*. NY: W.W. Norton, 1967.

Weatherford, Jack. *Indian Givers: How the Indians of the Americas Transformed the World*. NY: Crown Publishers, 1988.

Weisbrot, Robert. *Freedom Bound: A History of America's Civil Rights Movement*. NY: Penguin, 1991.

Wellman, Carl. "Terrorism." *Violence, Terrorism and Justice*, R. G. Frey and Christopher W. Morris, eds. NY: Cambridge University Press, 1991.

West, Cornel. *Racematters*. Boston: Beacon Press, 1993.

Wilber, Ken. *The Atman Project*. Wheaton, IL: Theos Publishing House, 1980.

———. *No Boundary*. Boston: Shambhala, 1981.

Wilhelm, Richard, trans. *The Lao Tzu Tao Te Ching*. London: Penguin-Arkana, 1985.

———. trans. into German. *The I Ching, or Book of Changes*. (English translation by Cary F. Baynes.) NJ: Princeton University Press, 1990.

Williams, Cecil. *No Hiding Place*. San Francisco: HarperCollins, 1992.

Wolman, B. B. *Contemporary Theories and Systems in Psychology*. NY and London: Plenum Press, 1981.

Yalom, I. D. *Existential Psychotherapy*. NY: Basic Books, 1980.

Yutang, Lin, ed. *The Wisdom of Lao Tse*. New York: Modern Library, 1948.

Zinn, Howard. *People's History of the United States*. NY: Harper & Row, 1980.

———. *Declarations of Independence*. NY: Harper & Row, 1990.

AUDIO AND VIDEO SOURCES

Barsamian, David, 2129 Mapleton, Boulder, CO 80304, 1-800-444-1977, Alternative Radio/New Tapes.

Boston University, Krasker Memorial Film Library,
    565 Commonwealth Ave., Boston, MA 02215, 617-353-3272.

Chomsky, Noam. "International Terrorism: Problem and Remedy."
    2/8/87 David Barsamian, 2129 Mapleton, Boulder, CO 80304,
    1-800-444-1977, Alternative Radio/New Tapes.

Davis, Agnes, "Liberty and Justice for All?" Boulder, CO, 2/15/91.

Engel, Barbara. "Reform and Revolution the Soviet Union." 9/27/91.
    David Barsamian, 2129 Mapleton, Boulder, CO 80304, 1-800-
    444-1977, Alternative Radio/New Tapes.

Graham, Mary interviewed by Caroline Jones. "Aboriginal
    Perspectives, ABC." Search For Meaning, Radio Tapes From
    Radio Programs, GPO Box 9994, Sydney 2001, Australia.

Johnson, John. "The Edge in Relationships." Common Boundary
    Conference Tape, 1992, CC12, The Common Boundary, MD.

Halprin, Sara. "Chronic Symptoms," 4-Part TV Series. Process
    Works, Lao Tse Press, P.O. Box 40206, Portland, OR, 97240-
    0206.

——— . "Process Work, Addictions, Conflict." 4-Part TV Series.
    Process Works. Lao Tse Press, P.O. Box 40206, Portland, OR,
    97240-0206.

Mindell, Arnold. "Worldwork with Michael Toms" and "Dream-
    body with Michael Toms." New Dimensions Radio, San Fran-
    cisco CA.

——— . "Process Oriented Psychology." Thinking Allowed
    Productions, 1-800-999-4415, Fax 510-548-4375 or -4275

——— . "Coma, Working with the Dying." Thinking Allowed
    Productions, 1-800-999-4415, Fax 510-548-4375 or -4275

Mao By Mao, Anneberg Cpb Collections, a BBC Film in the
    Pennsylvania State Film Library.

Marable, Manning, "Building Multicultural Democracy." 11/2/91
    David Barsamian, Alternative Radio, 1814 Spruce, Boulder,
    CO, 80304.

Mbiti John S. "African Religions and Philosophy." Nairobi &
    London: Heinemann, 1992.

Parry, Danaan. "Warriors of the Heart." Bainbridge Island, WA.
    Pennsylvania State University Audio-Visual Services, Special
    Services Building, University Park, PA 16802, 614-863-3100.

Parenti, Michael. "Marxism and the Crisis in Eastern Europe." 4/90
    David Barsamian, 2129 Mapleton, Boulder, CO 80304,
    303-444-8788, Alternative Radio/New Tapes.

Reagon, Bernice Johnson. Keynote Address for Common Boundary
    Conference Tape, 1992. The Common Boundary, MD.

Sagen, Carl. "Black Holes and the Future of the Universe." 120-
    minute Public Broadcasting System production.

——— . "The Creation of the Universe." Public Broadcasting Com-
    pany.

Said, Edward. "Nationalism, Human Rights, and Interpretation." Washington, D. C., 4/29/92. David Barsamian, 2129 Mapleton, Boulder, CO 80304, 303-444-8788. Alternative Radio/New Tapes.

Ture, Kuame. "Black Nationalism." 2/28/90. David Barsamian, 2129 Mapleton, Boulder, CO 80304, 303-444-8788. Alternative Radio/New Tapes.

———. "Black History." 3/2/92 David Barsamian, 2129 Mapleton, Boulder, CO 80304, 1-800-444-1977. Alternative Radio/New Tapes.

Williams, Chancellor. "The Destruction of Black Civilization." Chicago: Third World Press, 1987.

Zinn, Howard, "Democracy, Dissent and Disobedience." 12/88. David Barsamian, Audio Tapes from Alternative Radio, 2129 Mapleton, Boulder, CO 80304, 1-800-444-1977.

———. "A People's History of the U.S." David Barsamian, 2129 Mapleton, Boulder, CO 80304, 1-800-444-1977, Alternative Radio/New Tapes.

———. "Second Thoughts on the First Amendment." David Barsamian, 2129 Mapleton, Boulder, C0 80304, 1-800-444-1977, Alternative Radio/New Tapes.

RECOMMENDED MAGAZINES

Common Boundary, Bethesda, MD.

Cooperation and Conflict, £27/yr., £54/2 yrs., Sage Publications, 6 Bonhill Street, London EC2A 4PU.

In Context, Box 11470, Bainbridge Island, WA 98110. Issue 25, "Sustainability: the State of the Movement"; Issue 33, "We Can do It: Tools for Community Transformation"; and Issue 11, "Living Business: Turning Work into a Positive Experience."

Journal of Conflict Resolution, Sage Periodicals Press, 2455 Teller Road, Newbury Park, CA 91320.

Journal of Humanistic Psychology, Sage Publications, Newbury Park, CA 91320. Special Peace Issue, 32: 4, 1992, with articles by Simon Harak, Donald Rothberg, Brewster Smith, Stephen Kierulff, Melissa Johnson and Michael Newcomb, Mary Gomes, Neil Wollman and Michael Wexler and Alan Nelson.

Journal of Peach Research, £29/year, £58/2 yrs. Sage Publications, 6 Bonhill Street, London EC2A 4PU.

Journal of Process Oriented Psychology, The Lao Tse Press, P.O. Box 40206, Portland, OR 97240-0206. Subscriptions, $20 year.

New Dimensions Radio Magazine, San Francisco, CA, edited by Michael and Justine Toms.

New Age Journal, Brighton, MA.

The Nation, Box 10791, Des Moines, IA, $44 a year.

The Progressive, $3/issue, PO Box 421, Mount Morris, IL 61054-9938.

Race Traitor, $20/year, New Abolitionism, Box 603, Cambridge, MA 02140.

Reconstruction, $25/year, 1563 Massachusetts Ave., Cambridge, MA 02138.

Security Dialogue, £29/ yr., £58/2 yrs., Sage Publications 6 Bonhill Street, London EC2A 4PU.

Sun: A Magazine of Ideas, 107 North Robertson St., Chapel Hill, NC 27516, 919- 942-5258.

Tikkun: A Jewish Critique of Politics, $31/yr., P.O. Box 1778, Cathedral Station, New York, NY, 10025.

Thinkpeace, $25/yr., Oakland, CA 94609, 510-654-0349.

Tricycle, The Buddhist Review, $20/yr., Box 3000, Denville, NJ 07834.

Utne Reader, P. O. Box 1974, Marion, OH 43305, $18 a year, bimonthly.

World Policy Journal, New School for Social Research, 65, 5th Ave., Suite 413, NY, NY 10211. $26/year, quarterly.

Z Magazine, 18 Millfield St., Woods Hole, MA 02543, 617-236-5878.

Index

abuse and 114
as a drug 49
as double signal 57
awareness of 49, 61, 225, 229
conscious use of 53, 64
defined 28, 42
economics and 167
facilitation and 29
heterosexual 51, 69
hierarchy and 37
in conflict 40, 137
in facilitation 136
in group process 181
in relationship 69
in worldwork 18
indicators of 51
influence on communication
        style 42
international 56, 228
mainstream 51
male 51
marginalization and 64
national 50, 228
of People of Color 57
of Soviet Union 50
of whites 57
overt 58
parental 51
power and 49, 58, 137
privilege and 28
psychological 51, 59
racism and 151
relativity of 70
revenge and 75, 77, 88
self-esteem and 51
social 57
spiritual 59
submerged 58
terrorism and 75
types of 61–62
unconscious use of 77
white 51
reactions, symmetrical 81
recklessness, as characteristic of
        terrorism 96
reform
    defined 225
    relationship to revolution 226

relationships
    countercultural 71
    diversity in 66
relativity
    of concepts 45
    of rank 70
    social 45
religion
    as indicator of rank 62
    politics and 180
    views on human rights 132
religious persecution 60
repression
    democracy and 232
    of racism 154
    of rank issues 154
    of timespirits 207
    through revolution 228
resolution
    discussion of 136–137
    of social problems 86
    through processing roles 85
respect, as goal of terrorism 100
retaliation, as phase in group pro-
        cess 169
revenge
    as last resort for disenfran-
            chised groups 124
    as modus operandi 86
    as wake-up call 76, 80
    awareness training in 87
    causes of 77
    double signals of 79
    dynamics of 229
    facilitation of 81, 86
    for childhood wounds 87
    in foreign policy 86
    key to transformation 87
    power of 174
    rank and 88
    relationship to rank 75
    signs of 79
    social injustice and 78
    terrorism and 75
revolution
    against mainstream 40
    as means to be heard 33
    as result of marginalization

ABOUT LAO TSE PRESS

Lao Tse Press is dedicated to publishing information about Taoism and Process Oriented Psychology. Founded in 1988 as Process Press in Zurich, Switzerland, it publishes the *Journal of Process Oriented Psychology*. Joseph Goodbread's *Dreaming Up Reality* and the re-publication of his *Dreambody Toolkit* are forthcoming.

The Journal of Process Oriented Psychology and books by Arnold and Amy Mindell are available from Lao Tse Press. Write for catalogue: P.O. Box 40206, Portland, OR 97240-0206.